njuta

njuta

(Enjoy, Delight In)

The Swedish Art of Savoring the Moment

NIKI BRANTMARK

creator of *My Scandinavian Home*

HARVEST

An Imprint of WILLIAM MORROW

All illustrations ©GoodStudio/Shutterstock, except pages 3, 240 ©K N/Shutterstock; page 10, ©Iliveinoctober/Shutterstock; page 12, ©Happy Job/Shutterstock; pages 20–21, ©Natallia_Chernova/Shutterstock; pages 36–37 and 124–125, ©Yuliya Kim/Shutterstock; pages 58–59, 68–69, and 184–185, ©Anastasilia Gevko/Shutterstock: pages 80–81, ©Betelejze/Shutterstock; pages 89, 100, 103, 164, and 218, ©Mallinka1/Shutterstock; pages 89, 100, 103, 164, and 218, ©Ajay Shrivastava; pages 35, 48, 55, 56, 74, 104, 116, 177, 183, 186, 210, and 215, ©OliaGraphics/Shutterstock; page 98, ©niyoseris/Shutterstock; pages 101, 196–197, and 213, ©Elena Pimukova/Shutterstock; page 119, ©Anastasiya Iljina/Shutterstock; pages 166–167, ©Maria Skrigan/Shutterstock; pages 192–193, ©Alex Tanya/Shutterstock; page 203, ©Adam Hoglund; page 205, ©pixelliebe/Shutterstock; page 214, ©svekloid/Shutterstock; pages 219–220, ©Stislow Design.

HarperCollins books may be purchased for educational, business, or sales promotional use. For information please email the Special Markets Department at SPsales@harpercollins.com.

FIRST EDITION

Book design by Stislow Design

Library of Congress Control Number: 2023935698

ISBN 978-0-06-328408-1

23 24 25 26 27 IMG 10 9 8 7 6 5 4 3 2 1

For Dad, who loved the simple things in life

contents

"Fear less, hope more; eat less, chew more; whine less, breathe more; talk less, say more; love more; and all good things are yours."

—Swedish proverb

SWEDEN IN A SNAPSHOT

- Located in Northern Europe, Sweden shares a border with Finland and Norway
- Country length: 1,000 miles
- Total country area 204,035 mi² (fifth largest in Europe)
- Population: 10,452,326
- Capital city: Stockholm
- Highest mountain: Kebnekaise (6,877 feet)
- Number of national parks: 30
- Around 68 percent of Sweden is forest
- 2,000-mile coastline with 30,000 islands
- 95,700 lakes larger than 328 feet x 328 feet
- Home to 47 species of mosquitoes

MARMELAD

HALLÅ

STOCKHOLM

GOTHENBURG

MALMÖ

an introduction to
njuta

In recent years we've spent more time at

home than ever. For a period of time, our living space also became an office, a school, and even a gym. Visiting the nearby park, woodlands, or beach replaced holidays with exotic faraway places. And socializing has, let's just say, been distant! The COVID-19 pandemic was a big change for many across the globe, and even those who were fortunate enough to avoid serious illness struggled with the transition to staying indoors. But for the Swedes? Not so much!

You see, our Nordic friends are masters at finding balance, with *lagom* (not too much, not too little—just right) central to the Swedish psyche and society as a whole. But more than that, they are highly adept at gleaning delight from the simple things in life. They take time to relish that first sip of coffee in the morning, stop to feel the heat from the sun on their face, and cozy up indoors with a candle while a storm rages outside.

Ultimately, I've learned from my Swedish contemporaries that it's in the small things where greatness lies, and that it doesn't take a grand gesture or vast amounts of money to believe that life is not only okay but truly magnificent. They've taught me that small, simple, meaningful pleasures are all around us, every minute, every hour of the day if only you take the time to stop and consciously appreciate them. To feel good. To experience well-being. To njuta.

Glossary of some different forms of the verb *njuta:*

Njuter—I njuta
(can also mean you njuta or they njuta)

Ska njuta—I will njuta

Skulle njuta—I would njuta

Har njutit—I have njuta'd

Skulle ha njutit—I should have njuta'd

Njöt—I njuta'd

Hade njutit—I would have njuta'd

Njut—Njuta!
(a command or imperative)

Njutning—Njuta-ing

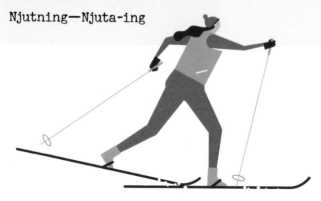

What is njuta?

Last January I headed out to the forest on cross-country skis for some much-needed "me time." Just as I arrived, a text message with one single word from my Swedish father-in-law pinged on my phone: "Njut" it read. I smiled. The one-word message served as a reminder to take in the beauty of the moment—the landscape, the silence, the solitude, the dappled sunlight over the tracks—and breathe it in.

Deriving from the old Norse *njóta* (to enjoy, to keep, to use), and pronounced "nyuutah," njuta is often translated to English as "enjoy," but that word falls short; it lacks the intensity and emotional value.

Swedish friends describe njuta as a personal moment where your body and mind are in complete harmony, and you experience the world in a positive way. It could occur in the blink of an eye or if you're lucky, a little longer. It can be as spontaneous as a cup of coffee in the spring sunshine: "When you enjoy a coffee and you njuter, you're consciously enjoying the smell, the taste, the warmth of the cup in your hands, the beauty around you—everything," interior designer Jannice Wistrand explains. Or as another acquaintance, Erik Blohm Nygren, described: "Reading a book under an apple tree on a summer's day."

Other times it might be the reward you get from exerting yourself. The wonderful feeling you get after a cold-water dip, or the sheer satisfaction and joy from summiting a mountain, soaking up the view, taking in the solitude, the silence, and the world at your feet. It might also be something you've longed for, like the taste of a juicy, crimson strawberry ripened from the sun.

To njuta is to savor a suspended moment in time without pressure or demand.

While it's commonly associated with the present, Swedes tell me you can also njuta over a joyful experience from the past or in anticipation of an exciting event in the future. Either way, to njuta is truly personal—and although it requires solitude for some, others might also experience it with loved ones with whom they feel truly relaxed.

The positive merits of training our minds to be in the now have been well documented by scientists. And well-being activities like yoga, mindfulness, and meditation have become increasingly popular.

But there's a relatively new kid on the block in the field of positive psychology. Coined in 2007 by Bryant and Veroff[1] as "savoring," the model involves "attending, appreciating, and enhancing positive experiences that occur in one's life."[2]

This is a model the Swedes have been inadvertently practicing for centuries.

To njuta is so ingrained in Swedish culture, it's simply a part of everyday life. And lest you forget, there's always someone around, like my father-in-law, to remind you: slow down, relax, nourish your soul from everything around you. Njut!

In a stressed-out, busy world, where there's a constant demand for our attention, it's easy to delay moments of gratification. As a London girl, I've been used to jumping from one task to the next, promising myself that I'll njuta after I've cleaned the house, made that call, flopped into the deck chair on vacation . . . But I've learned from my Swedish friends it's the tiny things in life that bring joy—and if you don't stop to appreciate them, you'll miss the magic.

I hope this book serves as a helpful reminder to take intentional pauses here and there, look up, and savor the moment.

Why njuta?

Alarming results from a global survey by Gallup in 2022 have shown that the world is more stressed and unhappy than ever before.[3] The pandemic certainly contributed to this, but even so, negative emotions have been on the rise since 2011, and Americans are experiencing the lowest levels of happiness in fifty years.[4] In essence, we're experiencing more negative experiences and fewer positive ones, as well as feeling more stressed, sad, and worried.[5]

The good news is much of what is needed to make us happier is right in front of you! Psychologists have found consciously savoring the moment to be a great tool in enhancing resilience and well-being.[6] By paying more attention to the world around you and how it positively affects your thoughts, your feelings, and your body, you'll create small pockets of happiness and get more out of daily life.

Best of all? To njuta doesn't need to take a long time, nor does it need to cost anything. To njuta is to find joy in the small, immaterial things in life. It's simply to seize the moment, make a conscious effort to stop what you're doing, and appreciate what's already there!

And there's another reason

Have you ever had a job appraisal that has been full of positive feedback, followed by a couple of areas of improvement—only to walk out and ruminate over the latter? Or perhaps you're walking along the street and out of nowhere you remember a mortifying moment from your teenage years, reliving the cringeworthy episode all over again. You're not alone! Humans are hardwired to focus on negative events—a phenomenon referred to as the *negativity bias*.

Negativity bias is likely a result of evolution. Being aware of danger has historically been essential for survival, and those more alert to threats were more likely to live, thus passing on the negative bias genes to their ancestors![7]

Thankfully, we no longer need to be on high alert quite like our ancestors, but we're still programmed to focus on the negative. This means we need to work harder to shift our focus to the positive—and create small, enjoyable moments in life to treasure and feel gratitude for! To njuta.

It takes practice and a conscious effort. For some, there might be a level of guilt, with putting yourself first seen as self-indulgent or shirking other responsibilities—and nothing pours cold water on njuta like worry!

Of course, to njuta shouldn't be at the cost of others. Swedes are an incredibly considerate, hardworking bunch—and everyone is expected to pull their weight for the collective good of society. It wouldn't go over well if you're reading a book under an apple tree while everyone else is pulling the cart! But at the same time, everyone understands the importance of resting and recuperating in order to be more efficient when you return to the task.

Furthermore, physical well-being is drummed into us from a young age, and others are fully supportive, even impressed by physical endeavors. And rightly so! But looking after mental well-being is lagging, and it's time to change the narrative. If you find yourself feeling guilty for taking a moment to yourself, remember that in case of an emergency on an airplane, you're told to put your own oxygen mask on first before assisting others. The reason? If you run out of oxygen, you won't be able to help others.

So, friends, it's time to set aside time in life for personal positive experiences, it's time to njuta more—for your own well-being and happiness—and in order to be a greater support to others.

The *livsnjutare*

In Sweden, there are people who like to relax and savor the moment, and then there are people who *really* like to relax and savor the moment. Enter the *livsnjutare* (someone who enjoys luxurious things in life such as good food and drink)!

Livsnjutare is often used in jest, but my twelve-year-old daughter Alice describes a livsnjutare as "someone who enjoys life as part of their daily routine. For example, waking up early and watching the sunrise, doing yoga by the ocean, and generally taking the time to do things you enjoy throughout your day."

To me, a livsnjutare moves through life much like a cat—a creature that loves to laze in the sun and take naps at will. To savor each moment is second nature and ingrained in their psyche so they don't even have to think about it. Feel like reading a book? Why not throw in a deck chair and a glass of rosé.

How great does that sound? In my mind, a livsnjutare has figured out the meaning of life, so if it doesn't come at a cost of others, sign me up!

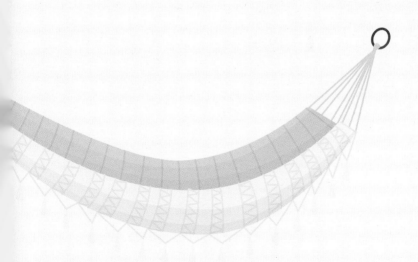

njuta

in daily life

> "All animals, except man, know that the main meaning of life is to savor it."
>
> —Samuel Butler, novelist

My brother-in-law, Johan, recently described his week like a washing machine—he enters the barrel on Monday before being tossed around all week and then spat out like damp laundry on a Friday, rung out and disheveled! Hopefully, not everyone's working week is quite as . . . um . . . tumultuous as this. Even so, daily life can have many demands on us, and it's easy to get caught up on a hamster wheel—always just barely keeping up, the same dinner thrown on the table, the same chores to be done . . . you get the gist!

The good news is, there's plenty that can be done to pep up everyday life and snatch small, positive moments to savor. It could be as simple as taking a different route or mode of transport to work, creating a wonderful atmosphere for an ordinary weekday meal, or celebrating the end of a project with a slice of cake!

But first, you need to get in the right mindset.

Make a list of the small moments that make you feel good

Pour yourself a coffee (Swedish style), put your feet up, and think. What are the small things in your daily life that give you energy and make you happy? Could it be cycling through the park? Could it be sitting under a tree, reading a book? Stopping to breathe in the ocean air on your way to work? List all the things that come to mind.

_____

_____

_____

_____

_____

_____

_____

_____

_____

_____

_____

_____

_____

A little extra effort goes a long way

"Add a golden edge to your every day."
—Swedish proverb

Now that you have a list, it's time to make a conscious effort to do more of these things you love—or at least stop to savor small moments during your day. But why not go that extra mile? As any Swede will tell you, to *really* njuta requires a little extra effort. Effort that will pay off!

Instead of simply crashing on the sofa, how about putting in a little effort to elevate the moment? As my friend Malin Persson advises, "If you take a few extra seconds to create a nice ambience, maybe dimming the lights, lighting a candle, and unfolding a blanket *before* you flop on the sofa, your contentment levels will soar."

Likewise, my friend Emma Mazhari doesn't just get home after a long day at work and plop herself down with a coffee; she'll make herself a latte, place it on a tray with a few cookies, and head out on to the patio with a cushion under her arm, before sipping her hot drink in the late-afternoon sunshine, looking out over the garden. "It's about pausing and resetting after a long day and taking some time out for myself before the 'evening shift' begins," she says. "I get so much energy from it."

Keep a look out for opportunities in your day to grab a few minutes for yourself and think carefully about what would give you the greatest pleasure at that moment. Take inventory of your surroundings to see what's missing and what you can add to really elevate the moment. Think about all your senses and how they can be heightened. Do you need to make it more comfortable by adding a blanket or cushion? Or perhaps dimming the lights or playing some soft music might make a difference?

Use your time wisely

Most of us race through the week, just barely keeping up, lamenting "there simply aren't enough hours in the day."

And yet there are others, like Malin—who works full-time, is a mother of three, and still has time for baking, preserving, and gardening. "You need to be incredibly careful with your time and prioritize how you use it," she advises. "It's easy to sit and scroll mindlessly and before you know it, half an hour has passed. In that time, you could have prepared the dough for a fresh loaf of bread for the next day." To me, that sounds like a great way to relax and be in the moment—plus, you'll really njuter from the taste of it the next day (see page 45).

Despite it being an incredibly precious resource, there can be a lot of spare time in the day to njuta—if only you use it wisely. Here are a few ways to free up those extra seconds, minutes, or even hours:

Stop scrolling so much According to Statista, an online platform specializing in marketing and consumer data, the average time spent on social media worldwide is 147 minutes per day.[8] If you were to cut that time down by even 60 minutes a day, you'd create seven more hours in your week to do with whatever you choose! When you do scroll, exercise "digital nutrition" and treat your online consumption like you would a healthy, balanced diet—less sugar, more fruit, and vegetables! In other words, while it can be fun and relaxing to watch humorous skits, social media algorithms make it easy to get lost down a rabbit hole and before you know it, half an hour has passed. Balance out mindless scrolling by proactively seeking out long-form content that reflects your passion and interests. Also, keep an eye on your screen time, turn off notifications, put your phone out of sight when you're not using it, and never take your phone into the bedroom (it's time to bring back the alarm clock). By using your phone less, you'll look up more, and be more present.

Stop procrastinating You know what you want to do or what your goal is, and yet there you are, doing everything *except* that. This is me before I go jogging—turning a quick thirty-minute jog into a one-hour extravaganza of torture! Do you recognize this? If so, try to turn your thought process on its head: prioritize a task, remember the reward you will get from it once it's done, and tell yourself that you'll have earned more worry-free time to relax afterward, safe in the knowledge that your task is complete!

Be more organized Nothing wastes your own time like being disorganized. I used to be the messiest, most disorganized person in the world (my family maintains I still am). But living in Sweden I have learned so much from my Swedish friends and colleagues who tend to be structured, organized, great planners, and all-around incredibly efficient. I mean, they even number their weeks, referring to weeks using a simple one to fifty-two system as opposed to spelling out lengthy month and week of references. A little effort in organizing your life goes a long way to making time for the things you love.

Be punctual In Sweden, being late is an absolute no-no. And although for me it took, um, some adjusting to, it certainly makes sense. I understand that by being more punctual—or better still, early—everything will run more smoothly, and you'll gain more time in your day. Oh, and you won't waste other people's time either. More time to njuta all-round!

Stop multitasking In a Swedish office you'll rarely catch people chatting or eating lunch at their desk. They save this for the break (of which they enjoy many—see page 173). If you look at the science, they're on the right (single) track. Many perceive multitasking as an efficient use of time, but research indicates it is actually less productive than tackling one task at a time.[9] If you really want to carve out more time to njuta, multitasking won't cut the mustard. And when you do sit down to enjoy a moment, you need to focus on your surroundings. So put down those tools (most important your phone) and be present, you'll get so much more from the moment!

Balance your expectations

Now that you've sussed out how to create more time for njuta, the next step is to figure out how to use those extra minutes/ hours in the best way! We have so many opportunities in life these days that there are choices to be made. And this can be overwhelming!

"The world is your oyster," "you can do anything if you put your mind to it," "go big or go home" . . . how often have you heard these phrases? They're said with the best intentions—but what does this mean? Should we travel at every opportunity, go out every night, and swing from the chandeliers? Learn a new language perhaps?

Having high expectations in life can be helpful in achieving goals and boosting productivity, as well as helping you to learn new skills. However, a plethora of studies has indicated that having constantly too high expectations from life can lead to disappointment, anxiety—and even depression. And crucially, it distracts you from the present.

In my mind, Swedes have a very balanced view of life—while they can aim high, they are also accepting of the lows. Lowering expectations doesn't mean leading a substandard lifestyle; instead, it helps us to maintain focus and be grateful for what we do have, not what we don't have. So, *ta det lungt* (take it easy). The answer is right here, right now. Sometimes you don't need to do anything at all except savor what you already have!

Don't sweat the small stuff

"Worry often gives a small thing a big shadow."
—Swedish proverb

To njuta requires quieting the active mind so you can fill your senses with the beauty of your immediate environment. In life, there are natural ebbs and flows and it's normal for us to worry about things. Swedes are known for staying cool and calm in bigger situations—and they barely notice smaller grievances. In my role at a major corporation in Sweden, I witnessed quite a few errors, some of them costly. I was surprised to find that rather than getting stressed and pointing fingers, they were met with soothing words such as *det löser sig* (it will work out) and *det är vad det är* (it is what it is). They might even say *ingen fara, det är ingen ko på isen* (no worries, there is no cow on the ice—i.e., no immediate danger).

Complain to a Swede about a small grievance and you might well hear a singsong *ja ja jaaaaa*—a sign to chill!

Put simply, Swedes don't tend to sweat the small stuff—at least openly. And this makes sense. When we become stressed, our body releases hormones that give us an energy boost—which is great if you need to flee from a situation, but not so great in daily life. Stress hormones raise your pulse, make you feel more anxious, and cloud your judgment.

This, I'm convinced, is why Swedes appear so calm, spending less time running around in circles and worrying themselves silly, and more time "doing," which in turn means a calmer outlook on life and, crucially, more time to njuta!

Worry is often about what might happen in the future or mulling over negative things from the past and keeps you from savoring the good things in the present. Make a mental list of all the things in your life you have to feel grateful for; it's a great way to focus on the positive.

Lower your expectations of others

I recently asked my mother-in-law, Christina, about her greatest lesson in life: "To have no expectations of others," came the quick reply. I was somewhat surprised. To be honest with you, it sounded like a bit of a downer!

"It's something I learned from my mother," Christina went on to explain. "After I left home, my mother didn't expect me to come and see her, so when I did, she was thrilled. On the other hand, if I didn't have the time, she wasn't disappointed or sad, she simply went on with her life as she had planned." This not only had a positive effect on her mother's well-being as she never felt disappointed or let down, but it also had a positive effect on Christina's life as she felt less pressure and demands. "I live by this today with my sons and in other areas of my life. I am so grateful for this life lesson."

Thinking about it, Christina *is* one of the most content people I know. She lives her life much like a cat: seeking out cozy spots in her home to read a book or knit. She loves to putter around, she loves to drink coffee on her balcony in the sun, and she loves to catch up with friends or go and see local exhibitions. And she is thrilled when we visit!

Perhaps we should all take a page out of Christina's book. Put simply, not having expectations of others gives you a sense of autonomy over external factors that you can't control–leaving more room for njutning!

Learn to say *nej*

"Better an honest no than an insincere yes."

—Swedish proverb

While lowering our expectations of others is one thing, we also need to learn to carve out time for ourselves, which can also mean setting boundaries. Saying "no" is no easy task and can leave many squirming (myself included)! Don't get me wrong, I love to socialize, but it's also important to take time out and restore my batteries. Stuck for the right words to decline and end up relenting? I've noticed my Swedish friends often use the phrase: "Unfortunately it doesn't work for me this time." It's polite yet firm, you don't get wrapped up in excuses, and it doesn't open any opportunity for discussion!

Now, where's that book I was reading?

Make time for alone time

"There are far fewer people who suffer from loneliness than enjoy it."

—Stig Johansson, Swedish-Norwegian linguist

To njuta is a personal experience. It's about you and your immediate surroundings and allowing the positives from your environment to fill your senses. It, therefore, requires time alone.

Unless you live alone, finding a little solitude is surprisingly tricky to do in this day and age—even if you're good at setting boundaries! Firstly, we are always connected via our phones, and then we have society to deal with—the world simply isn't built for introverts. Social behavior is rewarded, whereas enjoying a little alone time can be perceived as antisocial!

Not in Sweden.

Swedes show the same respect for people who choose to do activities alone—whether that's heading outside for a coffee in the sunshine or going for a hike—as they do for people engaging in couple or group activities. Want some me time? There's no need to explain, you're simply given the headspace to use your time as you please without judgment.

"I have lunch by myself, and I can go and have a drink by myself. A lot of Swedes do that. It's not strange; no one frowns," Carina Grefmar, an upholsterer with whom I share my studio, tells me. "Social distancing has never been a problem. We're not antisocial—it's just normal to enjoy one's own company. I am a very social person, but no one can be sociable all the time. You need time alone to recharge and simply be yourself."

This can also be seen in the way Swedes approach relationships—with *gift* (married), *sambo* (live-in partner), and *särbo* (live-apart partner) all acceptable norms. In fact, the Swedish word for married (gift), is the same as the word for poison—read into that what you will!

Swedes recognize time alone as an important way to *återhämta* (recover mentally and physically and regain your balance) and therefore highly respect anyone who wishes to do it alone. Here's why we should be following suit:

THREE REASONS WHY ME TIME IS IMPORTANT

1. **Being alone gives you space to reflect and allow your mind to wander, which inspires creativity.**[10]
2. **Research has shown that actively pursuing time alone for reflection and contemplation leads to positive emotions like relaxation and creativity, as well as finding greater pleasure and meaning in life.**[11]
3. **Being alone gives you time to get to know yourself and tap into your own passions and desires without influence from others.**

Don't feel guilty about carving out time for yourself to sit quietly and enjoy the world at your own pace. If all else fails, open a can of *surströmming* (fermented herring) and you'll quickly clear the area!

Do not disturb

If you love to chat with random strangers, Sweden isn't the place for you! Don't get me wrong, they'll politely respond, it's just that striking up a conversation with strangers is not done.

Why is this? "We're a large country with a small population.

We hate small talk and we're terrible at it," my friend Ullis Sjöström explains. "It's uncomfortable–I mean, how many times can you talk about the weather with a stranger?" Fair point, I guess. "We value our own space; we tend not to live too cramped, and no one puts pressure on you to chat. People are very respectful of others' personal space. We don't want to intrude and interrupt their mood or thoughts."

Furthermore, it's so nice and *quiet* too! Our Nordic friends are highly concerned about disrupting the peace of others and prefer to talk in soft, hushed tones as well as avoid noisy interludes such as loudspeakers in public.

It makes sense. After all, it's far easier to enjoy the simple moments in life, like sitting by the ocean on a sunny day and feeling the warm breeze on your face, if someone next to you isn't having a loud conversation about what they got up to last night or pumping out tunes from a boombox!

More njutning all around.

> ***Did you know . . .*** Swedes are incredibly conflict-shy, but push them far enough, for example by making copious amounts of noise and destroying the peace, and they might just go *skogstokig* (forest crazy) and claim *du har satt din sista potatis* (you have planted your last potato)! You've been warned!

CHAPTER 2

njuta

from food and drink

"Healthy body, healthy mind"— isn't that how the saying goes? According to the Bloomberg Global Health Index 2019—which looks at factors such as health risks like tobacco, obesity, high blood pressure, availability of clean water, average life expectancy, malnutrition, and causes of death—Sweden has an average life expectancy of almost 83 years, 69.6 years of which are considered "healthy," securing a respectable sixth place in the list of healthiest countries in the world (the U.K. occupies the nineteenth spot and the U.S. languishes in thirty-fifth place).

But how exactly does being healthy help you to njuta? Many Swedes tell me that to appreciate a moment, you need to feel comfortable. And this starts with the very basics: ensuring that your physical needs are met. After all, you're not going to be able to relax if you dying of thirst or your stomach's grumbling!

Eat well, live well

"Let the food silence the mouth."

—Swedish proverb

It's quite unbelievable how often food and drink come up when Swedes describe their njuta moments! Given that we eat at least three times a day, that's a huge amount of potential to njuta right there. But sadly, in our fast-paced lives, most of us non-Swedes mindlessly rush through our meals, gobbling down our food on the fly!

Sixty-two percent of Americans eat lunch at their desk,[12] and around 25 percent eat some type of fast food every day.[13] That's a lot of mindless munching!

So how can we njuta more from food? According to Swedes, it comes down to everything from the ingredients to how we elevate the occasion, taking pauses between mouthfuls and consciously appreciating every morsel. Oh, and don't forget to treat yourself every now and then too!

Cooking as an art form

Who knew that as an adult you'd need to think about what to eat every single night and, worst still, head to the supermarket after a long day of work? With three hungry teenagers in the house, cooking at home is usually done under duress too! But speaking to my friend, interior designer and foodie Bettina Kapare, there might be a way to turn this around.

"I love to indulge in cooking," she says. "I have tons of inspiring cookbooks, which are a joy to look through, and I'll flip the pages until I find the perfect in-season recipe, play some nice music, and maybe pour myself a glass of wine before I begin. I see cooking as a moment to relax."

Bettina is not alone. When I walk past Swedish homes in the evening, the lights are dimmed to a warm glow and the atmosphere is calm, unhurried, and harmonious. Perhaps if we all take this approach there might just be a master chef hiding inside us after all.

Savor the flavors of the season

These days we can pick up just about any food item year-round. But buying out-of-season produce doesn't do much for the palatte—or our wallets! Furthermore, a Swede will tell you, if you allow yourself to long for something, it will taste all the sweeter when it lands on your plate!

There's a science to back this up. Have you noticed that the first sip of your favorite ice-cold beverage tastes the best? This is because we adapt to pleasurable things, a phenomenon referred to as "hedonic adaptation." By abstaining for a period of time and allowing ourselves to long for something, we increase our appreciation and the pleasure we derive from it in the future.[14]

You see, in Sweden, in-season ingredients are highly prized. In autumn, bushes and trees are weighed down by deliciously ripe plums, apples, blackberries, and other juicy fruits. And there's nothing like plucking them directly from the branches and baking a crumble on the same day. While winter is about hearty, warming, and nourishing stews, spring has a far fresher palette. Asparagus, green beans, and seafood make a welcome return to the Swedish kitchen. Spring also sees the start of the much-awaited new potato season. Highly anticipated, the first batch of the season can fetch up to as much as SEK2,000 (US$200) per kilo! Come summer, fish, new potatoes, and fresh crispy green salads are washed down with homemade elderflower cordial, while bowls of juicy strawberries and pearls of black and red currants await for dessert.

"If you eat something all the time, it becomes less special, whereas if you long for it and associate it with a certain season, when it's at its finest, you savor every morsel," Ullis enthuses. "It's so much more enjoyable if it's produced locally and you can picture the farm or orchard it comes from."

Invest time in finding recipes that embrace the in-season delicacies in your area. Grow your own or buy locally where possible to really savor the flavor.

Foraging

One of my first memories of Sweden was sitting in a friend's grandmother's kitchen wolfing down waffles smeared with *lingonsylt* (lingonberry jam) and great dollops of cream. The lingonberries were a product of an autumn harvest and had been carefully preserved to be savored throughout winter (not that there was much left once I'd finished).

Foraging is relatively common in Sweden—in fact, come late summer and autumn, you're likely to spot people bearing baskets of blackberries, cloudberries, chanterelles, and other delicacies. You'll know they're foraging, as they'll dart away the moment they see you, careful not to disclose the exact location!

Not only does foraging require focus, drawing you into the present, but nothing tastes more wonderful than the fruits of your search! "We did a lot of foraging as a child on the Bjärehalvön peninsula on the coast of southwest Sweden," Bettina reminisces. "And I still remember the delicious taste of blueberries still warm from the sun."

If you're lucky enough to arrive home with an overflowing basket, every mouthful of blackberry crumble and sip of elderflower cordial will take you back to the wonderful place where you found the ingredients!

If you are a foraging rookie, it can be hard to know what's edible and in season in your area—after all, it's not a secret people are always willing to share! Do some research at your nearest library or join a local guided tour; you'll be amazed at what you can find for free and will be an expert in no time!

Preserving

Vikings were some of the first to preserve food in Sweden in preparation for their long journeys. And the tradition has long since been maintained, especially in previous centuries when dehydrating, salting, curing, and pickling food was a necessity to get through the long harsh winter. This may not be the case today, but the tradition lives on in Sweden, with preserves such as pickled cucumber, beetroot, and herring used to elevate everyday snacks and meals.

"In Sweden, we have a short summer season and traditionally have a lot of fruit and berries growing in the wild. My grandmother taught me to make the most of this," Bettina says. "Rather than allowing the surplus to go to waste, I love to make jams and chutneys. When you bite into a jam sandwich made from your own preserves midwinter, it will immediately take you back to that warm summer's day and you relish every mouthful."

Making, bottling, and labeling preserves is a satisfying process, but the real reward comes from indulging in your concoction on a cold, gray winter's day. You'll be transported back to your sunny garden, or the autumn woods, conjuring up the wonderful feelings that come with it.

THREE POPULAR PRESERVES IN THE SWEDISH PANTRY

To get you started, here are three easy-to-make preserves to elevate even the dullest dishes! The recipes are widely available online.

1. *INLAGD SILL* (PICKLED HERRING) Traditionally found in abundance off the Swedish coast, sill (herring) has been pickled since the Middle Ages. Marinated in everything from mustard and dill to garlic and chili, pickled herring is commonly eaten on a sandwich or alone with potatoes and salad and is always included in Christmas and Easter smorgasbords.

2. *SMÖRGÅSGURKA* (SANDWICH CUCUMBER) You'd be hard-pressed to find a Swedish pantry without a jar of pickled cucumbers. This sweet yet salty delicacy is designed to elevate the simplest of open sandwiches and as a side (along with lingonberry) on Sweden's national dish: meatballs and mashed potatoes!

3. *RÖDBETOR* (PICKLED BEETROOT) No Swedish pantry would be complete without a jar of crinkle-cut pickled beetroot! Traditionally enjoyed as a beetroot salad with meatballs, atop pâté on crispbread, or with *Pytt i panna* (a potato, chopped meat, and onion dish like hash), this deep red delicacy is a hit with all ages.

Cook differently

We're creatures of habit, and unless you're a culinary pro, the stove, oven, or barbecue is likely your cooking appliance of choice. But why not try a brand-new recipe to slow down the process and savor something new?

Smoking fish

A few months ago, I arrived at my father-in-law's house in a small fishing village on the southwest coast of Sweden expecting a barbecue. Instead, he was shrouded in smoke. Bo was busy smoking salmon. *Varmrökt lax* (warm smoked salmon) is just many of the ways Swedes cook or preserve salmon—and not only is it delicious, but it also lasts for up to two weeks in the fridge. Why not get out of your barbecue comfort zone and invest in your own smoker? Since the odor of the fish smoke will keep others at bay, you'll have plenty of time to yourself to njuta—plus everyone will devour the salmon when you bring it to the table!

Baking bread

We've made breads and other doughy delights for centuries. And while it used to be out of necessity, there's something to be said for the slow process, the feeling of the dough between your fingers, and the scent of bread baking in the oven.

Kneading dough is extremely therapeutic and relaxing as well as an excellent way to be in the present. Little wonder it's a popular pastime among Swedes. "We're used to seeing our parents and grandparents bake bread, so it's natural that our generation also bakes—it's an important part of family life," Johan explains. "It's an easy skill to get good at quickly, and the process is a great distraction. You're fully focused on the task at hand. But best of all you can really njuta from the results. There's nothing better than freshly baked bread straight from the oven, with a pat of melted butter and a cup of coffee."

Maybe you're already on it, but if not, challenge yourself to bake a fresh loaf of bread or batch of *bullar* (buns) for breakfast this weekend. They'll be way better than any store-bought bread—and you'll look forward to your weekend breakfast even more!

Knäckebröd *(crispbread)*

"Hard bread makes the cheek red."

—Swedish proverb

We've been brought up to recognize "an apple a day keeps the doctor away"—but in Sweden, it's the crispbread that keeps you from your local clinic! Known as *knäckebröd* (meaning "bread that can be broken"), the hard, whole grain flatbread has been a staple in Scandinavian homes for centuries. Known as poor man's food, knäckebröd traditionally comes from central Sweden and was made twice a year— once during the autumn harvest and a second time in the spring, and dried and stored on a rod above the stove (hence why it often has a hole in the center) for up to a year at a time.

Today, crispbread continues to be enjoyed across the country as an open-style sandwich, topped with slices of cheese, pâté, or hummus (as well as a touch of pickled preserves—see page 44). If you'd like to enjoy the crispbread crunch, February 19 is the day earmarked for celebrating it in all its glory!

It's not just what, it's also how and where

A few months ago, a friend and I climbed a fell (a mountain above the tree line) in Norway. Potentially a little unprepared (I'll forever be grateful for those clear mountain streams, which meant I could quench my thirst) and way out of our comfort zone, we were hugely relieved to finally trudge back into the village. We celebrated with a cool beer in a fjord-side bar. Nothing has ever tasted better. As I recounted this to a Swedish friend, she pointed out that if I had drunk the same brand of beer at the same temperature from the same glass elsewhere, it wouldn't have tasted anywhere near as good.

The difference is we had worked for it and longed for it. The beer was our reward. Likewise, nothing tastes better than when my family and I grill hamburgers in the woods over an open fire midwinter (see page 100). The ingredients might be the same as perfectly ordinary hamburgers we barbecue in our backyard in the summertime, but after a long, cold hike we savor the flavor like never before!

Much like foraging or cooking or baking something from scratch, even the simplest of food and drink can taste incredible simply based on the effort that goes into getting it into your hands—and/or the environment/occasion in which you consume it. In my experience, Swedes like to keep meals simple, choosing to elevate the occasion rather than the food itself—a great way to go!

Did you know... comparing and reflecting on how an experience is better than another one from the past or a different setting can enhance and prolong positive emotions?[15]

Choose the right tools for the job

While we're on the subject, Swedes also place great importance on the tools you use for your meal. Historic design brands such as Rörstrand and Orrefors make a regular appearance, naturally elevating the mundane and adding a touch of *vardagslyx* (everyday luxury) through porcelain and glassware. "What use is it in a cupboard or even hidden in the attic only to be used once a year, when you can roll it out on a weekday and enjoy it?" asks my friend Sofie Lejdström, who loves to buy crystal bowls secondhand (for a song!) and use them for evening meals. Mix and match different styles and eras for a relaxed look—and add a touch of nostalgia by adding pieces that have been passed down from generation to generation.

Get comfy

We are so much more able to njuta from moments if we feel comfortable. Do like the Swedes and soften up chairs and benches around the table with circular sheepskin mats and/or larger sheepskins draped over the back of chairs. If it's a bit chilly, you might also like to place blankets over chair backs, ready to unfurl. The extra effort will make everyone feel more comfortable—so that they'll come for the food and stay for the conversation!

Bring nature to the table

When it comes to table settings, Swedes love to keep things simple, aesthetically pleasing, and always practical! Bring in a touch of the season with flowers or foliage. Even one bloom can make all the difference, but you might also choose to make a statement with a huge branch!

Levande ljus (candles) are also an essential element, especially in darker months of the year. The warm, flattering glow sets the tone and adds a wonderful sense of harmony and togetherness at the strike of a match!

How to njuta more from every meal

The time of day calls for different types of refueling; even so, all meals are important, and with a little extra thought, you can njuta from each occasion!

Breakfast

In all my eighteen years living in Sweden I don't think I've seen a Swede skip a meal. *Frukost* (breakfast) is key, with savory continental-style ingredients such as bread, cheese, eggs, cucumber, and caviar the preferred choices. And just in case you miss it before heading to work, some of the bigger companies like to provide free breakfast (a safety net, if you will)! Nursery school children who arrive before 8:00 a.m. are also served breakfast. But there's another thing I've noticed: Swedes take a calm approach to the first meal of the day. And it's something they learn from a young age.

"At nursery school, we use breakfast as an opportunity to start the day in a serene way. We dim the lights, play soft music, and talk in hushed voices—it helps the children to learn to slow down and take their time to enjoy their food," my stepson, Albin, a nursery school assistant, tells me. "It also sets the mood for the rest of the day. If you eat a good breakfast, you're more able to tackle whatever life throws at you during the day."

FIVE WAYS TO ADD A LITTLE VARDAGSLYX TO YOUR MORNINGS

1. **Keep all the ingredients you need for breakfast on a tray (you might need one in the fridge and one in the cupboard). When you wake up, all you need to do is pull it out and everything will be in place, ready to go! It's quick to pack away too.**
2. **Prep the coffee machine the night before—you'll have fresh coffee at the press of a button.**
3. **Use your favorite cup—the one that's just the right size, looks beautiful, and feels great in the hand. Or maybe it just holds special memories. Either way, your coffee will taste all the better for it.**
4. **Play soft music or your favorite radio station and light a candle—small touches can make all the difference!**
5. **Shake up the location—eat on your balcony, in the garden, or by the ocean after your *morgondopp* (morning dip) (see page 113) if nearby! Or stop in the park on the way to work.**

Lunch

You should have seen Albin's panicked face when I pulled out a sandwich for lunch one day. "Great snack, when's lunch?" he asked.

At noon (maybe even 11:30), you'll see Swedes break down doors to get to their hot lunch! Preschools, schools, workplaces— there's not a place (if not in-house then just down the road) that doesn't serve a hearty warm, well-balanced lunch (a far cry from my English school lunch box involving a tuna sandwich, a bag of chips, a sugary drink, and a candy bar—my children still can't believe it).

While the Swedes might not njuter quite as extensively over lunch as people in some other European countries, like France, they still see its value. "Shutting down your computer, relaxing, and enjoying a decent lunch allows you to pause and reset. And it means you'll feel more energized and efficient for your afternoon shift," Ullis explained. Not only that, but the right food is also important, and the nutrient-rich Nordic diet hits the spot (studies have shown that people who eat a lot of nutrient-dense food report increased happiness and greater well-being).[16]

Why not treat yourself to something nutritious and delicious for lunch and savor each morsel? A little meal prep the night before does wonders to ensure you have a good midday meal waiting for you—and while you're at it, seek out a nice spot in the sun (preferably by moving water—see page 99). If you really want to go all out, go for LUS (*Lunch Utan Slut*, a long lunch that stretches into dinner) and you might just achieve livsnjutare status!

Dinner

The evening meal is a great time to relax and gather around to chat about your day. Why not make it extra special, Swedish style?

"We're all so busy these days that dinner has become a really sacred time," my friend Malin explains. "Rather than spending a lot of time cooking, I make big batches of food, so we have more time to set the table in a nice way, dim the lights, light candles, and make our evening meal feel really special—it's about creating an atmosphere that feels warm and comfortable. All electronics are set aside so that we can truly be in the moment."

Think about cooking in bigger batches so that you can save time not cooking on other days. It will leave more time in the evening for other things—and more time to njuta.

SEVEN WAYS TO ADD A TOUCH OF VARDAGSLYX TO DINNERTIME

Swedes have an amazing ability to surround themselves with beauty, and quite often it comes down to creating the right atmosphere. Here's how to spruce up your table setting for a touch of vardagslyx and njuta more from each mouthful!

1. Set the mood—avoid harsh bright lights and aim for a soft, golden glow instead, for a warm and relaxed feel. Candles are an instant mood lifter too.

2. Use a simple linen tablecloth and napkins for that little extra *lyx* (luxury). Did you know that you can spray a linen tablecloth with water when it's already on the table to remove all the creases?

3. Dig out your finest silverware, porcelain, and glassware! Using poor tools can distract from your enjoyment of each mouthful and the meal itself.

4. **Add in-season touches to the table to draw nature indoors (flowers, blossoms, or pine cones, for example).**

5. **Honor the ingredients. If they're homegrown, preserved, or from a farm, let that be known. (I'm not sure, though, that you need to say if it's from the supermarket!)**

6. **Be mindful of the smell and flavor.**

7. **Slow down and chew more so you appreciate each mouthful.**

As the Swedes say—*Smaklig måltid* (bon appetit)!

Wine tasting

Swedes don't tend to rush. They take their time to do things right, in an uncomplicated way. And their approach to wine is no different! It's not just about swigging back the booze (although you might witness this at a party), it's about creating a moment in which you can be completely in the moment. And for that, they need to set the ambience!

Gleaming wineglasses will appear beside a bowl of nuts, under the glow of candlelight. Swedes will wait patiently for the other person or people, without a *tjuvstart* (false start, or what I like to call a cheeky sip to test for corkage, of course). With all in place, there'll be a toast whereby glasses are raised to chin height (without clinking) and everyone looks into each other's eyes and says *skål* (cheers), then takes a sip. This will be followed by yet more eye contact and maybe a nod before setting the glasses on the table. And then the party (even if just for two) jumps to life again!

Why not learn more about wine (or your favorite tipple)? Sign up for some wine tasting courses online or in person. Take time to pick out wine, and familiarize yourself with the grape, region, and year—and ensure it pairs well with your food. You'll savor each sip more if you do! Don't forget non-drinkers, too, by ensuring there's a great option other than water!

Did you know ... despite Absolut vodka being a Swedish export, according to a study by CAN (Centralförbundet för alcohol och narkotikaupplysning, an organization monitoring alchohol and drug use in Sweden), 42 percent of the alcohol sold in Sweden is wine, over half of which is packaged in a practical bag-in-box format?[17]

Did you know... unlike Brits, Swedes never chat about how "wasted" they were the night before, even if they *were* wasted? To show off about how much you can consume is not really the done thing any day of the week, but you'd be particularly hard-pressed to find a Swede who would admit they drink on a weekday at all. But there's one exception: *Lillördag* (Little Saturday), which refers to Wednesday night—a perfectly acceptable time to take a midweek breather, head out, and enjoy yourself!

The Swedish *fika*

There is nothing more Swedish than a *fika*—taking a break and enjoying a hot drink (usually a strong coffee) along with a sweet treat. It's an institution, just like the British might enjoy an afternoon tea. The difference though is that a *fika paus* (coffee break) takes place multiple times a day—and can be enjoyed just about anywhere! In fact, it's estimated that a Swede spends an average of nine and a half days per year having a fika![18]

A simple, no-frills affair, a fika might involve the entire team at work, a quiet moment with your children at home, or stopping in the forest with your thermos. And it offers a perfect excuse to pause what you're doing, look up, and take in your surroundings. But best of all, it offers an excuse to savor a cinnamon bun!

Rather than drinking your mid-morning coffee on the fly, why not step away from the task at hand and really savor the moment—the taste, the smell, the feeling of the warm mug in your hands, your surroundings. Oh, and go on, treat yourself to that slice of cake too! You'll burn it off on your bike ride home anyway (see page 60).

CHAPTER 3

njuta

and exercise

I recently questioned Albin about njuta.

"I am terrible at sitting still and savoring the moment—my mind is so active and I'm always thinking about what's next," he lamented. "But there is *one* occasion: when I go for a jog by the ocean and then take a cooling dip. It's only then, while sitting quietly on the water's edge afterward without my phone, that I can truly njuta."

What Albin is experiencing is the endorphins that are released into your body after physical exercise and a cold dip (see page 112), which reduce your perception of pain and trigger a positive feeling in your body akin to morphine. The physiological impact of doing sports helps to quiet the mind, lowering stress and anxiety and boosting happiness, offering a fast track to njutning!

For some, like my restless stepson, Albin, exerting yourself in some sort of high-impact physical way is a fast track to calming the mind enough to relax and breathe in the moment.

Do you recognize this? If so, great. But in a time-strapped world, how do you carve out time for exercise too? The answer is to channel the Swedes and incorporate it into your daily life.

On your bike

The first stop is trading your car for a bike or simply walking. I have lived in Malmö for many years (hailed as the sixth-best cycling city in the world), so cycling has become second nature to me.[19] And I've shouted the benefits from the rooftop to my U.K.-based friends.

After all, they could use a nudge. According to Nesta, 59 percent of all car rides in the U.K. are less than five miles long—a distance that could easily be covered by bike.[20]

My sister Cas in London recently traded her car for a bike to use for her commute and hasn't looked back: "I love my daily commute by bike. It gives me the space to think, decompress, and clear my head to and from work, saves money, squeezes in exercise as part of my daily routine, and it's good for the environment. Plus, there's nothing more satisfying than cycling past long lines of traffic! I sometimes count the number of cars I overtake."

With bicycle-only lanes on the rise, biking will become easier and easier to do! You just need to have the right mindset and gear (including head-to-toe raingear and all the necessary safety equipment).

THREE REASONS WHY CYCLING HELPS YOU TO NJUTA

1. **Depending on the distance, your exercise is done for the day, giving you all the positive benefits that come with it.**
2. **You're more in tune with the season—the temperature of the air, the turning of the leaves from summer to autumn, the frosty mornings.**
3. **You're more present with the world around you: the buzz of people on the pavement, the jovial atmosphere on a sunny day in the park, children laughing, music playing.**

Invest in a bike with at least three gears and take inventory of your weekly activities. Which ones could you potentially walk or bike to instead? Perhaps it's your commute or the trips to and from school. Or maybe the grocery shopping or other small errands. You'll save money, get fit, and feel more closely connected to the world around you in the process.

Walk it out

Health-conscious Swedes also love to walk. Analysis of data by Stanford University found that Swedes take an average of 5,863 steps per day, while Americans take less than 5,000.[21] This could be attributed to walking as part of a daily commute, but also the popular *kvällspromenad* (evening walk). In Sweden, an evening walk in the great outdoors is a popular pastime, whether you have a pooch or not, helping our Nordic friends decompress and be alone with their thoughts after a long day.

Try a "savoring walk." Commit to a fifteen-minute stroll alone every day for a week, varying the route each time. Pay close attention to the positive things around you—the smells, the sounds, and the sensations. Not only will you feel energized, but it will also help to focus the mind and feel appreciation and gratitude for the here and now—and a 2007 study indicates you'll report greater happiness by the end of the week.[22]

For the love of sports

Exercise in Sweden isn't only confined to getting around by bike. According to a study by Eurobarometer in 2022,[23] an estimated 59 percent of Swedish adults exercise or participate in sports at least once a week (the European average is 38 percent), making Swedes the fourth-most active country in Europe. Jogging, tennis, soccer, basketball, handball, floorball, ice hockey, and skiing feature high on the list.

I appreciate their tenacity. After all, let's face it, after a long day at work, weighing up whether to enjoy a glass of wine or go for a jog is a no-brainer—one is painful, the other is a delight—at least in my mind! So just how do Swedes stay motivated? The key it seems is to exercise for the right reason.

Surveys have shown that while more than 60 percent of Swedes exercise to keep in shape, 50 percent exercise for fun, and only 20 percent exercise to lose weight.

Looking to up your game? Join a club!

I'm sure most of us agree that the best exercise doesn't *feel* like exercise. And this is so much more easily achieved if there's a social element involved. In Sweden, 30 percent of people are members of a sports club.[24] And they're certainly on the right running track. Research shows that by buddying up you're more likely to stay committed, work harder, and reach your goals. Best of all, you'll feel all the wonderful health benefits that exercise provides, leading to greater njutning!

Set yourself a goal or challenge

"To dare is to lose your foothold for a moment, to not dare is to lose yourself."
—Swedish proverb

For many years, my New Year's resolution was to "exercise more." I would last until about mid-February. And then one year I decided to set myself a more specific goal: to run 621 miles in twelve months. Being as stubborn as I am, it was all I needed to stay motivated, not least because people were following me on Strava (a fitness app that helps you to track your performance).

A physical challenge holds a huge amount of njutning. Depending on the task, you can really appreciate the planning and preparation phase, *maybe* the task at hand, but above all else, the moment you cross the finish line, open your thermos, bite into a cinnamon bun, and think "I did it." Many Swedes tell me they njuter from the memory and sense of achievement of completing a big challenge for years to come too!

What challenges are there in your area? Find one you like the idea of and then join a club or find a buddy. And don't forget to slow down and savor each part of the process—the planning, the practice, the actual event, and the afterglow!

The Swedish classic

"I have never tried that before, so I think I should definitely be able to do that."
—Pippi Longstocking

Every year, thousands of *taggade* (pumped) Swedes sign up to attempt *En Svensk Klassiker* (the Swedish Classic), a challenge involving the longest, hardest, and most historical races in Sweden. To gain their certificate, participants need to complete *Vasaloppet*, a 55.9-mile cross-country ski race, *Vätternrundan*, a 186.4-mile bicycle ride around lake Vättern, *Vansbrosimningen*, a 1.9-mile open-water swim (a third of which is upstream), and *Lidingöloppet*, an 18.6-mile cross-country run—all within twelve months.

It's grueling, no doubt, but Swedes who have completed the task tell me it's a thoroughly rewarding experience. I'm yet to be convinced, but I do understand the benefits. You'll of course be *vältränad* (as fit as a fiddle), learn new skills, see new places, and meet a lot of new friends along the way. "Every sport has a tremendously supportive community, both on and offline. There are so many people out there waiting to help you and you become a part of a wonderful community," Swede Yvonne Svea Gossner tells me. "Plus, it helped me to find a new passion. I had never tried cross-country skiing before I signed up for Vasaloppet, and now we go cross-country skiing every winter as a family. It's become one of our favorite activities."

The ultimate njutningen, though, comes from crossing the finishing line—the achievement is something you'll carry with you forever. "Every time I see my certificate, I feel a great sense of pride and relive the Swedish Classic all over again. It is something I will always be able to njuta from," Yvonne tells me.

I've heard they're already accepting entries for next year. . . .

CHAPTER 4

njuta

from hobbies

While exercise is great for the mind, body, and soul, it's not the only way to achieve greater njutning (phew!). My Swedish friends talk a lot about analog activities and how they help them to decompress and relax. Many have hobbies outside of the home that involve music and arts and crafts, all of which, they say, are a great way to be in the moment and reset.

Thank you for the music

When I was living in England, it didn't matter that I couldn't sing. The only time anyone would hear me would be at a birthday party, and even then I might lip-sync! But in Sweden they sing *all the time*. Birthdays, weddings, midsummer, crayfish parties, Christmas—any celebration provides an opportunity to belt out a tune!

In fact, singing is such a popular pastime that an estimated 600,000 Swedes (17 percent of the population) sing in a choir, which vary from the more serious church or academia choirs to the more relaxed "anyone can sing"–style setups (ABBA choir, anyone?).

"Choirs have a long history in Sweden," my friend Helena Gorne, a longstanding member of a choir herself, tells me. "They give you the chance to become part of a great community, giving you a sense of belonging. When you sing as part of a group, you are completely in the moment. It's something I njuter from."

"When I sing, I feel in total harmony with myself and my surroundings!" Ulla Stenlund, my hairdresser and a soprano singer in Eslöv Vokalensambel choir, tells me. "I'll arrive at choir practice after a long day in the salon, feeling exhausted, and I'll leave full of energy."

The Swedish government recognizes the benefits of singing in a choir too, listing it as a criterion for *friskvårdsbidrag* (a tax-free wellness allowance offered by employers for sports and other well-being activities).

It seems the Swedes are crooning in the right direction. Studies have shown that singing in a choir can lower stress,[25] help you better cope with emotional pain such as depression and grieving,[26] boost your immune system,[27] and even increase your pain threshold[28]—and might also reduce snoring.[29] (That's it, I'm signing up my husband, Per!) But best of all, you get to relax and belt out your favorite tunes.

Love to sing? Look for a choir in your area. Or set aside time to have a good old-fashioned sing-along in the car, at home, or at a karaoke bar—and keep a look out for sing-along cinema and theater performances. You might just surprise yourself at how much you enjoy it—plus you'll reap the rewards, whether you're in tune or not!

Play that funky music

Not many know that Sweden is the world's third-largest exporter of music, pumping out chart-topping tunes in every genre from pop and rock to heavy metal. ABBA, Avicii, Roxette, Robyn, Swedish House Mafia, The Cardigans, Ace of Base . . . the list of globally recognized bands is endless. Swedes are also ridiculously good at writing and producing music too: think "Baby One More Time" by Britney Spears (Max Martin), Kelly Clarkson's "Stronger (What Doesn't Kill You)" (Jörgen Elofsson), and "Poker Face" by Lady Gaga (Gaga and RedOne).

What explains this extraordinary output? One key reason is that musical talent is nurtured from a young age, thanks to government-subsidized music lessons. To give you an example, my daughter Olivia enjoyed weekly flute lessons for a song (sorry!) at Malmö Kulturskola, a municipal music school, for a term fee of $30, and a further $10 to rent the instrument itself.

"The government recognizes the importance of music," Per explains. "By subsidizing lessons, every child can learn a musical instrument and pursue their musical ambition no matter their background."

No matter how painful it might be to listen to your budding musician practicing their scales on a recorder (have your earbuds at the ready), the effort will pay off. A study by the Brain and Creativity Institute at the University of Southern California (USC) revealed music education in childhood assists language acquisition and reading skills.[30] And you might want to think twice about telling your kids to "turn that racket down." A study has shown listening to music during a math test can improve performance by 40 percent (so that's why I did so badly on my General Certificate of Secondary Education exam).

Better still, pick up an instrument yourself. Research indicates that making music can help to lower blood pressure and decrease your heart rate, helping you to decompress, as well as feel calmer and in the moment. The harmonica, guitar, ukulele, keyboard, and drums are thought to be some of the easier instruments to learn. Just saying!

Not up for playing? Studies have also shown that listening to music (even sad music) helps to reduce stress[31] and improve your mood,[32] inducing pleasure, joy, and motivation,[33] and helping you to feel more present. So book that concert, turn up at a gig, or crank that dial! And in the words of Roxette: *C'mon join the joyride!*

Why not set up a dedicated space at home designed purely for listening to music? All you need is a record player or stereo/Bluetooth speaker, some favorite LPs/CDs/Spotify playlists, great headphones, and a beanbag or an armchair with a footstool by the window. It's bound to become a favorite spot to njuta after a long day.

Did you know ... the audio streaming and media service Spotify was founded in Sweden in 2006 by Daniel Ek and Martin Lorentzon?

Get crafting

Sweden has a strong history of folk art, with decorative paintings in bold colors and embroidery featuring nature, people, and biblical motifs all a part of its heritage. Decorative glass and porcelain have also always had a strong presence.

"I cherish items all the more when I know they've been made by hand," my friend Sofie tells me. "Being around handicrafts and antiques helps one to feel a strong sense of connection to the item, its story, and Sweden's heritage as a whole."

Swedes love to *pyssla* (craft) as well as engage in hobbies such as pottery, painting, sewing, and knitting—some traditional crafts such as candle-making and rug weaving are also making a comeback. Researchers claim that repetitive, rhythmic activities using your hands such as these can calm the mind and help you feel more in the moment akin to meditation, as well as boost happiness and reduce stress.[34] There's a world of crafting opportunities out there, you just have to tap into the one that you enjoy the most!

There are plenty of online tutorials showing you how to learn a new art and make things from scratch. Better still, ask someone you know in your community to show you the ropes. I'm sure they'd be proud to share their knowledge and you might just make a new friend in the process. With a little practice you'll have a bowl, a wool sweater, or a pair of *raggsockor* (wool socks) (see page 208) to treasure in no time. Until then, hopefully, you'll njuta from the experience!

The power of clay

There's something wonderful about the gooey clay between your fingers and the hypnotism of the pottery wheel. In Sweden, pottery has a rich heritage dating back several centuries—and has enjoyed a big revival in recent times. Many of my Swedish friends are members of a workshop and throw pottery in their spare time. "I started taking an evening class and slowly got the hang of it," my friend Helena, an accomplished ceramicist, tells me. "I head to a community workshop several times a week to throw pottery. You can't think about the stresses of the day and be at the wheel or it will all go disastrously wrong! Pottery requires your full focus, there's a lot of precision involved! I love the output, but most of all, I do it because it's therapeutic."

Why not sign up for a pottery workshop and try your hand at it? Depending on what you're looking to create, it'll take patience and hard work, but your efforts will be rewarded!

Photography

I can't claim photography to be specifically Swedish, even if a Swede did invent the world's first single-lens reflex camera for medium format (the iconic Hasselblad 1600F)! Even so, being a shutterbug has an important place in this book.

"Photography helps you to focus and appreciate the beauty in your surroundings, the light, the scenery, and the magical details that might have otherwise passed you by," Swedish photographer Patrik Larsson explains. I feel better about the 37,484 images on my iPhone now!

Psychologists assert that setting aside time to take meaningful pictures significantly improves your mood and helps you to feel more appreciative and motivated.[35] Plus, if you frame a special moment in time, you can njuta from it for years to come!

Read or listen to a book

"A house without books is like a room without windows," wrote Henry Ward Beecher in *Eyes and Ears*, and he's right!

Apart from the wonderful escape, the wealth of knowledge, and the pure enjoyment you glean from a good book, research has shown that reading for thirty minutes decreases your heart rate, lowers your blood pressure, and reduces stress.[36]

Why not elevate the moment so you can really *njuta* by creating a designated reading corner? Swedes would employ a comfy armchair with a footstool, a good reading lamp, a small side-table for coffee, a candle, and a soft blanket to snuggle under! Silence, solitude, and a great book. What more do you need?

Sommarboken

Sommarboken (the summer book) is an initiative by public libraries across Sweden encouraging adults and children alike to borrow, read, and review a certain number of books over the summer. Those who complete the task are rewarded with a free tome. Plus, their reviews help others to find great reads too. Something to suggest to your local library?

CHAPTER 5

njuta

in nature

> "I took a walk in the woods and came out taller than the trees."
>
> —Henry David Thoreau, American naturalist, essayist, poet, and philosopher

With a country the size of California and a population of just over ten million, nature is never far away in Sweden. Mention that there's a body of water nearby and the Swedes are walking down the road in their bathrobes faster than you can say *bada* (bathe). And don't even get me started on the forest!

With Sweden's ever-changing seasons (and weather!), vast landscape, and the incredible "right to roam" (more on this to follow), Swedes have a deep connection with nature. Many are highly adept at identifying edible plants and mushrooms and recognizing birds just from their song as well as swatting away mosquitoes with a single swipe!

What's in a name?

So entwined are Swedes with their surroundings that even names are inspired by nature. My daughters have a Björn (bear), Sten (stone), and Linnea (twinflower) among their circle of friends. And surnames are equally nature related. My own name, Brantmark, means steep ground. And you'll have no doubt heard of these famous Swedes whose last names mean:

GRETA THUNBERG (environmental activist)—grass-grown mountain hill
ASTRID LINDGREN (writer)—lime tree branch
INGRID BERGMAN (actress)—mountain man
BJÖRN BORG (tennis player)—bear fort (both names together)

Friluftsliv (open-air life)

Despite 88 percent of Swedes living in towns and cities,[37] they work hard to maintain a strong connection with nature, with many frequently venturing out to enjoy activities in the wilderness, a pastime they refer to as *friluftsliv*. The term was popularized by the Norwegian playwright Henrik Ibsen, who recognized the importance of spending time in nature to increase spiritual and physical well-being in the mid-1800s. Today, the word is a regular part of the Norwegian and Swedish vocabulary.

If you go to the woods today, you'll encounter Lycra-clad hikers, joggers, and cross-country skiers zooming past in a blur, their ponytails swishing into the distance. Along the coast and around Sweden's waterways, you'll likely see kayakers, sailors, and swimmers gliding effortlessly along, or hear a tiny gasp as someone takes a *kallbad* (cold bath). But it's not just the energetic types who embrace green areas. The Swedish Folkhälsomyndighet (Ministry of Health) also recognizes friluftsliv as an important way to enjoy "more quiet individual encounters with nature that provide the opportunity for relaxation, recreation, and recovery."[38]

The right to roam, and respecting nature

Of course, it's easier to embrace nature if it's accessible. *Allemansrätten* (the law stipulating everyone's right to nature) gives the Swedish public the freedom to roam in the countryside by foot, bicycle, and ski, and to camp on any land except near a dwelling or on crops, ensuring that nature is easily accessible to all.

This freedom comes with a caveat: *Don't disturb—don't destroy.* Swedes highly respect nature and value its importance to clean the air we breathe, filter our water, and provide a home for wildlife.

As a result, Sweden has been featured in the top ten of the global Environmental Performance Index for more than a decade thanks to its clean air, clean water, and low emissions. There is of course work to be done, and the government has set ambitious targets to secure the future of our planet, which all Swedes are committed to achieving.

Why njuta from nature?

At a recent dinner, my *bordsherre* (the guy to my left) explained that to njuta you need to "disconnect," a tricky task in this fast-paced world. And the Swedes are emphatic that nature holds the key. "Heading out into the wilderness is to step out of your busy life and be rewarded with silence and solitude," my friend Nina Syde, a nature conservationist, explains.

"Nature places no demands on you. It doesn't care if you are there or not, it just carries on doing its thing," Ullis adds. The waves still travel to shore, the snow still falls to the ground, and the wind still blows in the trees. "When you allow yourself the time to simply sit and watch the rhythm of nature, your mind stills, and you feel immense calm."

The healing powers of nature

Over the years, the world has moved further away from nature. It's estimated that up to 56 percent of the world's population and 83 percent of people in the U.S. live in urban areas,[39] and it's projected that this number will double by 2050.[40]

As we adapt to city life, we'll become less and less in touch with nature—unless, like the Swedes, we put in the effort. That effort is especially important when we understand that nature is not a "nice to have" but essential to our mental and physical well-being.

Research indicates spending time in nature reduces feelings of anger, anxiety, and stress and can help soothe pain, improve focus, and evoke feelings of calm while boosting meaningfulness and vitality.

This is all well and good on a glorious summer's day, but if you're walking in a howling gale with horizontal rain or find that strolling in a dark forest gives you the heebie-jeebies, instead of wanting to run to the hills, you'll want to run home!

So just how do Swedes make the most of their time in nature—rain, snow, or shine?

Dress for the weather

I'm embarrassed to admit I showed up at my daughter's Swedish preschool gathering in white jeans, only to find it was an outdoor meeting under the boughs of a tree (even if it had been indoors, admittedly my attire was a poor choice). "Please sit down," the *fröken* (miss; title of respect for a woman) said. I looked down at the damp, muddy ground in a panic. Meanwhile, the Swedish parents obliged. I glanced around and realized they were all wearing *utebyxa* (outer trousers).

Worn over your usual trousers, these waterproof protective trousers are sturdier than rain trousers and allow you to enjoy the outdoors without fear of getting your clothes dirty or damaged—even if you are wearing white jeans underneath!

Swedes have learned from childhood that you are unable to *njuta* from nature if you're not dressed in a way that makes you feel comfortable and free. "If you're too hot, too cold, too wet, or worry about getting mud on your trousers, you can't relax and delight in your surroundings," my daughters' friend Edith explained. *Kläder efter väder* (dress according to the weather) is the Swedish motto. Here are four essential pieces of clothing Swedes would never venture into nature without:

1. **Layers of weather-appropriate garments that can easily be added or removed**
2. **A seasonally appropriate windproof/snowproof/water-resistant jacket**
3. **Utebyxa or winter ski bibs**
4. **Comfortable, waterproof shoes that you don't mind getting dirty, or snow-appropriate shoes with extra insulation**

Children and the great outdoors

"Children do as you do, not as you say."
—Swedish proverb

In Sweden, children spend a copious amount of time outdoors, exploring, digging, planting, playing, and experimenting. Some Swedish preschools (referred to as *utedagis*, or "forest schools") are outdoors only with a shelter for when it rains or snows! It's in these early years that the love affair and respect for nature begins, bolstering pro-environmental attitudes and compassion.[41] Do you have children? If so, help them to learn to appreciate the joys of nature like a Swede!

THIRTEEN WAYS TO FOSTER A LOVE AND RESPECT FOR NATURE

1. Always dress your child in weather-appropriate clothing so they can explore their environment without hindrance.

2. Allow your child to explore freely and play in nature.

3. Invite your child to join you when gardening or watering plants around the house.

4. Grow vegetables and flowers from seeds with your child.

5. Take your child on a nature trail through woodlands.

6. Take your child foraging.

7. Teach your child to recognize bird sounds, insects, and wildflowers.

8. Craft things together with your child from nature.

9. Teach your child how to identify leaves on a tree and enjoy making bark rubbings together.

10. Teach your child to respect nature.

11. Head out into the garden, the park, or the wilderness with your child no matter the weather.

12. Go on picnics with your child no matter the weather.

13. Teach your child about safety in the wilderness.

HOW TO MAKE LEAF ART

At a recent festival in Malmö, I stumbled upon a great way to make leaf art. Not only does the process help to release pent-up tension (it involves a hammer after all!), you'll also njuta from your artwork for years to come!

WHAT YOU NEED

- A tree stump or strong surface
- A square piece of muslin cloth
- A hammer
- Fresh leaves of your choice

STEPS

1. Arrange the leaves on the stump.
2. Place the muslin over the leaves.
3. Repeatedly hit the muslin with the hammer until an imprint of the leaves can be seen.
4. Take the muslin home and frame it.

Adopt the right mindset

It's one thing owning all the right clothing, but if you look outside and all you see is *ösregn* (driving rain), all you'll want to do is dive back under the covers!

But it's time to think differently.

Cas and I once booked a four-day sailing trip in the Norway fjords. On the morning we were due to set sail, we looked out to the sea on a gray, overcast day. I could barely see the fjords through the drizzle, and we huddled together to shield ourselves from the biting wind. "Are we really going out there?" I thought. Stepping reluctantly on board the catamaran hours later, we were handed an adult-sized onesie with a waterproof shell and a thermal liner. And as we sailed off into the drizzle, scuttling past skerries and islands, we forgot about the weather entirely and marveled at the spectacular surroundings.

Your effort to go out in adverse weather conditions will be well rewarded too: You'll have the wilderness to yourself, and you'll see it in an entirely beautiful new light. Plus, 99 percent of the time, it looks worse through the window than really is!

And even if you do end up getting cold or wet, you'll appreciate your home even more when you step back through the door. There's nothing quite like hanging your wet, wool socks over the fire and snuggling up on the sofa with a steaming mug of tea after being exposed to the elements. Njutning at its finest!

Learn to love the wilderness

How and what you njuter from is incredibly personal and you'll find yourself more relaxed in certain environments. "Although I find forests lovely, they are not relaxing for me per se, and certainly not somewhere I would choose to njuta," my mother-in-law, Christina, tells me. "I believe the type of nature we feel most relaxed in as an adult is deeply connected to our childhood. I spent all my summers by the coast, and today the beaches, cliffs, and rocky outcrops are somewhere I go to seek comfort and solace. My Finnish cousin, on the other hand, grew up by a forest, and it's there she feels at peace, wandering the trails and picking berries."

Just like Christina, every Swede can pinpoint a place where they feel most happy and content, and they have a word for it: *smultronställe*.

Smultronställe

Cas called me the other day and was telling me about her recent trip to Cornwall in southwest England. "I love it there so much," she enthused, "I just feel so happy and relaxed from the moment I arrive, and all my worries fall away." "Aaaah," my husband, Per, replied knowingly, "it's your smultronställe."

Directly translated as "wild strawberry patch," the smultronställe refers to a special place where you feel happy and relaxed and at your most content.

THREE STEPS TO FINDING YOUR SMULTRONSTÄLLE

Perhaps you already have a smultronställe in mind. If not, it's great to identify where you njuter most! When you close your eyes and think about a place outdoors where you are content, happy, and relaxed, what does it look like? Is it a beach, with the soothing sound of the waves lapping on the shore and the soft sand between your toes? Is it a cool, mossy green forest? Or perhaps it's up on the moors or the banks of a particular river? Try the following exercise to discover your special place:

1. Close your eyes and think back to a relatively nearby place where you felt completely and utterly relaxed and at ease with your surroundings.

2. Conjure up an image in your mind's eye of a beautiful place where you feel pure joy.

3. Recall sounds and smells that evoke happiness and contentment.

Make a note of the places or environments where you feel most at peace:

_____

_____

_____

_____

_____

_____

_____

_____

_____

_____

_____

_____

Plan to visit the places or environments you have listed (if far away, find similar landscapes nearer to you)—and ensure regular visits moving forward so that you can truly njuta.

Appreciating all kinds of nature as an adult

Knowing your smultronställe is a major plus; even so, it's never too late to learn to appreciate and even love other types of environments too. My friend Bettina, a Swede who lives in the French Alps, loves to hike up mountains and camp for the night by herself. As a city slicker, I looked at her in awe when she told me this. "Climbing a mountain and pitching a tent for the night is not something you do off the bat," she responded, taking in my surprised look. "You build up to it over time. I started hiking with friends and then camped over with them, gaining knowledge and experience of the terrain, as well as knowing the dangers and pitfalls and which gear to bring. Eventually, I had the knowledge and confidence to go it alone."

If you're new to a certain kind of wilderness, it can be a foreboding place, not to mention dangerous. Find a friend who loves the great outdoors and tag along or find a guide. It's a great way to get out of your comfort zone and learn something new, as well as build up your stamina and experience, without investing in tons of gear. There might just be a Bear Grylls inside you waiting to come out!

Njuta from the forest

The Brothers Grimm fairy tales like "Little Red Riding Hood" and "Hänsel and Gretel" would have us believe that forests are full of witches and wolves. And certainly there are wolves in Sweden (albeit shy ones). Even so, Swedes have a slightly different attitude toward forests than, say, some Londoners!

Growing up in the suburbs of London, I remember the woods next to our house being a dark, foreboding place, where the shadows would make me jump. I'd run through it, heart pounding, blood coursing through my veins, fearing the boogeyman would get me!

Tucked up in bed, I'd hear foxes scream and badgers scuttle about in the darkness, and rather than marvel at the magnificence, I'd think, "How nice to be all cozy in my bed and not out in that scary forest." What a contrast to my Swedish friends!

With Sweden being covered in approximately 68 percent forest,[42] you're never far away from it, and it's not unusual for children as young as six to be allowed to wander in the forest and woodlands by themselves. "When I was little my parents were happy with me playing in the small forest near our home," designer, founder, and CEO of Swedish Ninja, Maria Gustavsson, recalls. "If you think about it, forests are way safer than cities—there are no roads to cross, and rarely any people either. I used to love exploring the forest alone. It was full of fascinating things such as plants, berries, and mushrooms, as well as boulders and trees to climb. These days, my husband and I encourage our children to explore and have fun with nature too.

"Recently, some London friends rented a cabin beside the forest on the Danish coast, and we went to visit them for a few days," she goes on to relay. "Their children were bored and either on their screens or taking the occasional dip in the sea. They hadn't explored the forest at all. When we arrived, my children rushed off into the woods, climbed trees, built dens, and jumped from boulder to boulder. We barely saw them over the entire four days!"

Of course, city woodlands differ from forests in the far north of Sweden. "The forest isn't dangerous—unless, of course, it's home to bears and wolves—people are," Swedish visual designer Lucas Brusquini explained. "The further you are from civilization, the safer it becomes and the more you can relax. Even so, it's important to use the nature you have at your disposal to teach your children the wonders of it—and embrace it yourself!"

Forest bathing

While we all love a coffee and a cinnamon bun, Swedes will tell you that there are other ways to immerse yourself in nature! In recent years there's been much talk of forest bathing. A Japanese term that emerged in the 1980s, *shinrin-yoku* encourages one to take in the ambience of the forest. It's been hailed by scientists as a great way to disconnect from daily life and be more mindful of your surroundings.

Like the Japanese, Swedes fully understand the therapeutic effects of the forest on the mind, body, and soul. While we mainly focus on what we see, studies have shown that many of the benefits of nature are delivered through what we hear, feel, and smell.[43]

I've learned from my Swedish friends that there's a big difference between going for a simple walk in a forest and fully immersing yourself in your surroundings. To do the latter, you need to stop, look up from the trail, and truly soak up your surroundings. Breathe in the fresh mossy air. Marvel at the views. Appreciate the solitude and silence and truly embrace everything that nature has to offer.

Taking a break

This type of immersion is so important to a Swede that they'll nearly always pack a picnic, no matter the season. If you're thinking of a couple of sandwiches and a thermos of coffee, you're barking up the wrong pine tree. The Swedish pit stop requires a little more gear—after all, you need to be comfortable and warm to want to hang around and savor the moment for any great period of time, especially in the snow!

Essential pit stop gear

Seat pad I first discovered unassuming foldable seat pads when a friend pulled two out of her backpack on a walk soon after I arrived in Sweden. Fitting neatly in any small bag, when folded out these compact mats are just big enough to fit your derriere. And with waterproof and insulating properties, they help to protect your *rumpa* (bottom) from the cold, wet ground. Swedes are introduced to this handy piece of gear in preschool, and you'd be hard-pressed to find a backpack without one!

Tools to light a fire Scouts or outdoor adventurers might be adept at rubbing two sticks together to light a fire, but for the rest of us mere mortals (and most Swedes for that matter), matches or a lighter are a good idea!

Wide-mouth thermos Not up for barbecuing or unable to light a fire? Invest in a wide-mouthed thermos, fill it with boiling water, and add *wienerkorv* (thin frankfurter sausages). That way you can enjoy a warm hot dog in an instant!

Hand-carved wooden cup Originating in Lapland, the *kåsa* (referred to as *Guksi* in Sámi) is a type of drinking vessel traditionally crafted from birch burl by the Sámi people of Lapland. A popular piece of outdoor gear, a kåsa is lightweight, hard-wearing, and can withstand extreme temperatures, making it ideal for the Swedish climate. Due to the burl, adventures will leave their mark on the mug in the form of nicks and scratches. A sip of coffee from it will escort you straight back to an evening around the campfire.

Knife Many Swedes I've spoken to (particularly the men) list a knife as an important piece of equipment, not just for practical purposes but also to relax and connect with nature. My friend Mattias Lejdström always carries one on trips to the forest and has also taught his sons how to use one too. "We bought Harald and Hjalmar a children's version of a *morakniv* (a knife from Jämtland in the north of Sweden). When we stop for lunch or set up camp, we'd give them small tasks such as making kindling or *grillpinnar* (sharpening the end of long sticks so they could be used as spears for roasting sausages over the fire). They loved the challenge and still bring their knives with them today."

While carving can be relaxing, everyone should be aware of the dangers and follow certain rules:

1. **Always sit down calmly when using a knife.**
2. **Always carve away from you.**
3. **When moving around, always have the knife in a sheath.**
4. **Observe local laws with regard to carrying a knife.**

Back-to-basics lifestyle

It's funny how chores like cooking, boiling water, and washing up can feel so tedious at home yet so much fun in the wild. By setting up camp, lighting a fire, and cooking over a naked flame, you're stripping life back to the basics, to a time when our forefathers would live a simple hunter-gatherer lifestyle. When you're in touch with the wilderness, simple everyday tasks that feel like a bore at home become miraculously enjoyable and a great way to focus the mind and immerse yourself in the present.

Where to stop

Where possible, Swedes will choose to take a break somewhere they can light a fire. After all, there's nothing quite like the warmth and the meditative flames to help you feel relaxed, rosy-cheeked, and in the moment. Whether in a forest clearing, by the beach, or in your own backyard, lighting a *brasa* (fire) is an ideal way to stay warm and enjoy time alfresco.

My family and I have spent many a winter afternoon gathered around a brasa in the forest, roasting sausages on sticks. "The beauty of a fire is that it turns a hostile, uninviting environment into somewhere warm and inviting," Per explains. "Just because it's cold, it doesn't mean you can't enjoy a meal outdoors—it's impossible to not enjoy the moment, and the conversation always flows better around a fire!"

If you have the space, why not build a simple fire pit in a safe section of your backyard or find places in nature where you're allowed to light a fire and enjoy meals alfresco? "The key is to dress for the weather and keep it simple," advises Nina. If you prepare hot food, you'll be more likely to want to linger. "Grill sausages on long homemade spears or *pinnbröd* (bread twisted around a stick) before enjoying hot chocolate and marshmallows," she recommends. "After all, it's more about being cozy and in the moment rather than indulging in a Michelin star meal."

How to make pinnbröd

This classic "bread on a stick" savory snack is ideal to grill over an open flame with family and friends or alone. Beware though, it takes some practice to get it exactly right! "Most Swedes have tried it, most Swedes have failed miserably and burned it, and most enjoy it anyway because you're out in the wilderness," says Johan, laughing. "It takes longer than you think to bake, but your patience will pay off, and you'll relish the taste of the freshly baked bread with melted butter."

HOW TO MAKE GOLDEN PINNBRÖD!

INGREDIENTS

- 1 ³/₄ cups flour
- ¹/₂ teaspoon salt
- 1 ¹/₂ teaspoons baking powder
- ³/₄ cup water
- A very long, thin yet sturdy stick that's around ³/₄ inch in diameter

STEPS

1. Combine the flour, salt, and baking powder in a mixing bowl.

2. Add the water and knead it into a dough.

3. Divide the dough up into long ¹/₄-inch-wide pieces.

4. Tightly twist each piece around the stick.

5. Heat the pinnbröd over an open flame, turning it frequently. You know it's ready when it comes off the stick easily. Be patient, it can take some time—and be careful not to hold it too near the flame or it will burn.

6. Enjoy the warm bread as it is or add a dollop of butter!

Porridge

Looking to spend several days, weeks, or even years in the wilderness? To hardcore advernturers such as Markus Torgeby, who lived alone in a hut for four years in the forests of Jämtland, warming *gröt* (porridge) is the answer. It's simple to make (just add water), cheap to buy, easy to cook in one pot, and filling, plus it warms you up and you can add all kinds of foraged berries from the forest to change the flavor.

Slow coffee

While water is of course essential, as a nation of coffee lovers (Sweden is the sixth-largest consumer of coffee per capita in the world),[44] Swedes would never head off into the wilderness without it! While in the south, Swedes usually make coffee at home and carry it in a thermos; in the north, people enjoy a slower, more mindful approach: *kokkaffe* (boiled coffee).

Kokkaffe is the process of slowly brewing coursely ground coffee beans in water in a stainless-steel pot over an open fire while enjoying the quietness of the wilderness.

"It's important to be patient when brewing kokkaffe," my friend Sofie explains, having experienced the ritual on a trip to Lapland. "It's a slow process without a filter, so you need to wait for the sump to subside before you serve it." As with all njuta moments, your efforts will pay off. "Apart from the fact that the coffee is at its best, it's also cozy, atmospheric, and simple. It's a perfect way to tap into all the senses and enjoy your surroundings."

HOW TO MAKE KOKKAFFE

INGREDIENTS

- Coffee beans or pre-ground coffee suitable for boiling
- Fresh water
- Clean, fireproof coffeepot (preferably stainless steel)
- Log fire

STEPS

1. Coarsely grind the coffee beans.
2. Pour the ground coffee into the pot (approximately $1/4$ cup ground coffee beans per 4 cups of water).
3. Add fresh cold water.
4. Put on the lid and place the pot directly in the fire, on a grill over the fire, or suspend it over the flames from a carefully placed branch.
5. Bring the coffee to a boil and carefully remove it from the heat immediately (if it continues to boil it will quickly become bitter).
6. Stir well and allow to settle for 8 minutes or until the sump has sunk to the bottom before serving.

The mindful forest experience

While we all love to bite into sausages and sip copious amounts of coffee, there are plenty of other ways to immerse yourself in the forest too!

On a recent trip to our local *bokskogen* (beech forest), I discovered a marked *harmonirunden* (harmony trail), with tips on how to consciously experience well-being from the forest. Here are the six simple steps I learned:

1. **Find a quiet spot in the forest or woods where you feel calm and safe (let's face it, if you have a vivid imagination like I do, you won't be able to concentrate if you fear a bear might pop out at any moment, so do your research!).**
2. **Sit with your back against a tree and close your eyes. Take three deep breaths. Be mindful of how it feels.**
3. **Shift your focus to the skin on your face and think about how it feels. Do you feel warm or cold? Can you feel a breeze or small raindrops on your face?**
4. **Move your focus to your ears and listen to the sounds around you. What can you hear? The leaves rustling? Birds singing? Maybe even a deer treading lightly on the forest floor?**
5. **Open your eyes and look around. Can you see the sun through the canopy? Are the leaves quivering in the breeze?**
6. **Finish off with some deep breaths and let nature's scents fill your body. Sit and embrace your surroundings to the fullest extent while you relax.**

Did you know . . . tree hugging might be considered a sport for hippies, but they're, um, barking up the right tree? Studies have shown that touching a tree increases levels of oxytocin, the hormone responsible for emotional bonding, calming the mind, and overall well-being.[45] Not quite feeling the hippie vibe? Try casually reaching out and touching the bark and the leaves. Take in the changes of the season and sit with your spine against the trunk of your favorite tree to get all the feel-good vibes without the stares!

Find a glade

"There's an unexpected clearing in the forest that can only be found by the lost."

—Tomas Tranströmer, Swedish poet, psychologist, and translator

On a nice day, a forest glade offers the perfect place to stop in the forest. "I love to lie on the mossy floor and soak up the warmth from the sunlight that streams through the space in the trees. It's completely silent except for the gentle sounds of nature going about its work," Nina tells me.

Become a bird-watcher

Gökotta (cuckoo daybreak) is the Swedish ritual of getting up early to go outside and listen to birdsong. It specifically refers to cuckoos in the springtime, but you can enjoy it at other times too. I did so on a recent walk in the forest by my cottage, where Ullis and I stopped dead in our tracks because there was a woodpecker working his way from tree to tree, tapping away. We probably wouldn't have seen him had it not been off-season when wildlife dares to venture nearer to the beaten track. We stood dead still, barely daring to breathe. We were completely focused on the moment and all our thoughts and worries simply disappeared as we marveled at his work.

While this was only fleeting, it's a memory that remains with me. Bird-watching has a nerdy reputation, but these days I recognize something magical about observing and listening to the song of our feathery friends. And unsurprisingly, it has a profound effect on our mental and physical well-being, with studies associating bird-watching with evoking feelings of relaxation and calm.[46]

It also helps us to feel more connected to our surroundings. It's heartwarming when the same bird blesses you with their presence. I for one love the sight of a particular little, round, red-breasted robin who stops by our patio to say hej each day! He forces me to stop, focus, and admire his puffed-out breast before he flutters off again to go about his busy day!

Think about becoming a bird-watcher! Get to know the birds in your area and learn to recognize them by appearance and sound. "Birds are most active in the early hours, so it's best to be out and about from dawn, regardless of the weather," a Swedish family friend and birdwatcher enthusiast Bo Häggström tells me. "The bird-watching community is very generous when it comes to spreading information about what they see and where—and all ages are welcome!"

You won't believe the drama that plays out in the canopies should you stop long enough to pay attention. Plus, you might just make a new feathered friend. Njutning all around!

Vindskydd *(open-sided shelters)*

In Sweden, you'll find *vindsykdd* dispersed along most trails. Simple structures made from wood, they provide an open-sided platform on which to sleep, a grill and ready-chopped wood or an axe of some kind to chop your own, and a picnic table. All you need to bring is your sleeping bag, food, and drink, and you're all set for a night in nature (or at least a lovely pit stop during the day!).

No access to a ready-made shelter? It's quick and easy to build a *koja* (den).

How to build a koja

Building a koja is an activity enjoyed by children, rain or shine, and it also makes for a great shelter in *ösregn* (downpours). The good news is you don't need any rope or equipment. All you need to do is to collect long, sturdy branches from the forest floor and lean them up against a tree trunk at a 45-degree angle, circling the tree as you go. Stack as many branches as you need to protect yourself from the wind and the rain.

Wild camping

While visiting nature can be beneficial to your mind, body, and soul, there's nothing quite like staying for several days (some would argue weeks or, like Markus, even years). After all, to truly be able to relax and njuta, my Swedish friends explain, you need to be relieved of all pressures and demands.

"Walking in the woods is a great way to hit the pause button, but spending several days out in the wilderness is an entirely different experience," Ullis, a keen camper, tells me. "Life is stripped back to the bare basics and becomes a rhythm of lighting a fire, cooking, eating, drinking, sleeping, repeat—you become completely relaxed and in the moment. You also become in tune with the patterns of nature, the weather, the sounds, the smells, the scenery. It's the perfect way to reboot."

Thanks to *allemansrätt* (the law stipulating everyone's right to nature) offering the freedom to set up camp anywhere except on farmland or near a house, wild camping is a popular pastime in Sweden. And community services like Fritidsbanken, a nonprofit organization that loans out free gear including tents, sleeping bags, camping stoves, and anything else you might need, make it accessible for all.

Markus, the author of the books *Under the Open Skies* and *Sova Ute* (*Sleep Outdoors*), says it's vital for everyone to sleep outdoors every now and then. "We lose something if we always sleep in a temperature-controlled room with four walls and a ceiling," he explains. "Something happens to us when we're surrounded by infinite space. It gives us perspective. During the four years I lived under a cotton canvas in the Jämtland forest, I felt calm in a way I've never experienced before. I've never felt as much as I did during that time, and I've never enjoyed anything as much."

Camping rookie? Rent gear or tag along with friends or a guide who can show you the ropes, and head out for a night or two in the wilderness. Even if it's not for you, it'll be an experience you'll never forget and you'll njuta even more from the warmth and comfort of your own bed when you return.

Winter camping

Think camping is a summer activity? Think again! I recently met Wendy Sadler Hartlen who had moved here from Florida. As she was from a humid, subtropical climate, I was curious to hear how she coped with the long south Sweden winter. "I used to detest it," Wendy confessed, "and then my Swedish boyfriend introduced me to winter camping." Taken aback, I delved for more information. "We head out in all weathers on the weekends, barbecue, and sit around a campfire before settling down for the night in a special double sleeping bag. There's something wonderful about the stillness and solitude. It's the perfect antidote to everyday life, and it's transformed my approach to winter. Just don't forget to lay an insulated pad under your sleeping bag or you will freeze!" she explained. Worth a try?

SIX RULES FOR STAYING SAFE IN NATURE

While nature can be awe-inspiring, it can also be a dangerous place if you get caught unprepared. In Sweden, children are taught what to do if they get lost in the forest (lay three sticks across the trail and hug the nearest tree until help arrives) and anyone who lives in an area where bears and wolves roam free knows to make plenty of noise to not be caught off guard.

The weather is also an important factor. As a sailor, I was raised to respect the ocean. I am only too aware that what might look like a calm, sunny day in the morning can quickly change into a wild storm within hours.

Here are six rules to follow to ensure you njuter from your adventure without being caught unprepared:

1. Use a reliable source to check the weather forecast: always take heed of weather warnings and adverse conditions.

2. Tell others about your plans including your route and when you expect to return.

3. Dress for the weather (including layers that you can add or remove) and take all the necessary equipment for your adventure.

4. Plan your route, download a local app, and take a map and compass.

5. If you are new to the area, ask local experts for advice.

6. Keep to marked trails so you can easily keep track of your direction and how far there is left to go, and where you can access overnight cabins as well as call for assistance when required.

Bear necessities

There's a gentle rustle in the leaves as the dappled sunlight warms your back. Birdsong rings out from the canopy overhead and in the distance, you can hear the calming, gentle trickle of water from a stream. Suddenly, there in front of you is a bear. A great big, brown bear, one of around 2,500 wild bears in Sweden.[47] Some might say you're lucky (it's rare to see one)— although I'm sure at that moment, you'd beg to differ. Sweden's largest predator (although they also have a penchant for berries), brown bears can weigh up to 772 pounds.

You freeze, your heart pounds, and your instinct is to turn and run to safety. But in Sweden's backcountry, another tactic is required, one that goes against all instincts. On the official Sweden website, you're advised to strike up a conversation with the bear; speak in calm, gentle tones, clap your hands, and let the bear know you're there. And then back slowly away without turning your back or breaking into a run.[48]

Njuta by the water

The immense coastline and tideless waters surrounding Sweden make the coast and lakes a paradise for beachgoers, kayakers, sailors, stand-up paddlers, windsurfers, and practitioners of just about any other water pursuit you can imagine. But there's one pastime that's a national institution: bathing.

Swedes are so passionate about bathing that there is an entire vocabulary dedicated to water immersion!

Glossary of Swedish bathing terms

Badkruka—someone who doesn't like swimming in perilously cold water (I am apparently one of these)

Badkultur—bathing culture

Isbad—taking a dip through an *isvak* (a hole cut through the ice)

Kallbad—a cold dip in the lake or ocean (often preceded by a sauna)

Kurbad—a warm bath infused with natural herbs or oils

Kvällsdopp—an evening dip, enjoyed around sunset to rinse away the stresses and strains of the day

Morgondopp—a dip very first thing in the morning to set you up for the day

Nakenbad—to bathe without clothes

Premiärdopp—the first swim of the season

Varmbad—warm soak in a bath (often at a **varmbadhus**—a facility with baths)

Vinterbad—a dip in the lake or ocean in winter

Wild swimming

"One never regrets a bathe."

—Swedish proverb

Who doesn't love the idea of swimming in nature? In some parts of the world, the relatively new phrase "wild swimming" is used. For a Swede, it's simply to bada or bathe. Either way, bathing under the open sky surrounded by nature does wonders for your health, alleviating stress, soothing aches, and pains, and helping to restore your inner calm. Little wonder Swedes enjoy it as a daily ritual.

Visit a body of water in Sweden and you'll quickly spot someone arriving at the bathing deck in a bathrobe and clogs—perfectly acceptable attire, adding a spa-resort feel to small coastal villages up and down the country (they'll even stop at grocery stores on their way home to buy breakfast and no one will bat an eyelid).

Most bathing spots sport a thermometer bobbing at the bottom of the ladder, and word of the day's water temperature quickly spreads. It's important information as all Swedes are familiar with the temperature at which they feel is passable for a premiärdopp. Most Swedes prefer to bathe in the summertime, but there are some hard-core year-round bathers too (a wool hat is added to the robe/clog getup). Either way, given, the northern trajectory, the water can be pretty chilly, but pretending to be nonplussed is a national pastime for Swedes and you won't hear a single gasp!

Bathing is a ritual passed down from an early age, with a morgondopp often a family affair. The youngest Viking in our family, Alice, is probably the hardiest of all—throwing herself into the ocean in the snow, rain, or sunshine, all year round, while I boldly wait on shore with her towel (I haven't been blessed with Viking blood after all). But she particularly loves to bathe in the summertime all day long!

Nonchalant they may be, but the benefits of bathing don't pass by the Swedes. "There's something wonderful about the scenery, the way the water tastes, how it clears the mind and makes you feel alive," Per tells me. "If you skip a dip, it's like skipping a morning coffee—you just won't feel the same all day."

Another keen bather, Ullis adds, "The ocean demands nothing of you, it just carries on as if you're not there, but when you go in, it embraces you—and you become a part of it, weightless, relaxed, and present. There's no feeling quite like it."

HOW TO NJUTA FROM WILD SWIMMING IN THE SUMMERTIME

1. **PLAN** Find your nearest safe outdoor bathing spot and inform someone of your whereabouts. Always be aware of the dangers—make sure the water is safe and tell someone where and when you are going and when you will be back.

2. **BEFORE** Simply looking at a large body of water can have a hypnotic effect and help you to wind down. Take a few moments to appreciate the scenery, the color, the shape of the water, and the clouds scuttling across the sky as well as the salty scent of the ocean and the sounds of the waves. It will never be the same again.

3. **DURING** If it's a warm day and the water temperatures are mild, dive down, taste the salt and minerals, and feel the coolness against your skin.

4. **AFTER** *Man ångrar aldrig ett bad* (one never regrets a bathe) is Per's favorite saying. And it's true. No matter how stingingly frigid the water is, you will feel wonderful afterward as your blood rushes to warm up your blotchy limbs and soothe your pain. To make the most of the moment, leave your phone at home, bring some warm clothing to put on afterward, and pay attention to the feeling in your body.

5. **TAKE SOMETHING HOME WITH YOU** Why not prolong the feeling by taking a smooth pebble or shell home with you as a reminder of your morning dip? Every time you touch it, it'll bring back a hint of that moment of calm— something to njuta from!

Winter bathing

While summer bathing in Sweden can be chilly, a vinterbad is next level—falling firmly into the "no pain, no gain" category of njutning.

There's not really a limit to how cold Swedes will go. Ocean frozen over? No worries, we'll just create an isvak. Taking an isbad is not for the fainthearted. The freezing water causes you to gasp involuntarily (although not for a Swede, it seems!), and your body starts to pump out adrenaline. Your heart pounds and your initial reaction is to get the bleep out of there. So why do Swedes do it?

While they don't exactly enjoy the moment they're submerged, the ability to njuta afterward is immense! The cold causes hormones in the brain to kick in to soothe pain, which simultaneously makes you feel euphoric (not unlike morphine) and contributes to the post-swim high. The good news is, if you do it regularly, your body will start to adapt and react less to the cold, making it easier to stay in for longer—which in turn is thought to make you less reactive to everyday stress as a whole.[50]

A cold-water swim also helps you to feel connected to nature during the winter when we so often gravitate indoors, and can help lift your mood, improve memory, and ease tension and fatigue[51] as well as boost the immune system.[52]

But best of all, there's nothing better than climbing out of the water, donning a big cozy bathrobe and wool socks, and feeling that wonderful post-dip high surrounded by the elements.

Ready to dive in?

SIX TIPS FOR ENJOYING A WINTER DIP

1. **If it's very cold, wear a thermal hat and swimming or surf shoes. Swedes also swear by wool socks, which they keep on throughout the bathing experience.**

2. **Enter the water slowly and work on calming your breathing.**

3. **Don't feel the need to dip your head.**

4. **Wear something loose-fitting and warm like a cozy bathrobe with a big hood, long sleeves, and deep pockets so you can wrap yourself up the moment you get out.**

5. **Change into dry socks and slippers or clogs when you come out of the water.**

6. **Bring a thermos of coffee, tea, or hot chocolate (or something stronger!) to enjoy at the water's edge while you feel the wonderful effects of your cold-water effort on your body—and take in the beauty of your surroundings, as well as commend yourself on your bravery!**

Bada bastu

While winter bathing is relatively popular, many more Swedes prefer to *bada bastu* (sauna and then dip in the ocean) in the colder months of the year. In fact, it's an institution! Everyone in Sweden has access to a sauna in some shape or form. No matter the style, the idea is the same: total relaxation and rejuvenation through the process of bada bastu—heating up the body and then rapidly cooling it down in cold water—before resting and repeating the cycle again (up to three times).

The sauna is often considered a social place and somewhere all ages and walks of life are welcome. My parents-in-law book one for our extended family before we celebrate Christmas, Easter, and Midsummer (bathing suits are thankfully required on these occasions), and one of my friends, Malin Nihlberg, recalls happy memories of taking weekly saunas with her family as a child. Above all else, it's a great way to relax and reboot.

"I revel in the simplicity of it—the wind, water, fire, wood, sun, nakedness. Everything is stripped down to the elements," Leah Roth-Howe, a fan of Ribersborg Kallbadhus—the public sauna in Malmö—enthuses.

Looking to hit the pause button? There's no better place than a sauna. Cooling off in the cold winter is a shock to the system, but if you focus on your breathing, you'll stave off that fight-or-flight instinct and a wonderful sense of calm will wash over you. The greatest njutning, though, comes from relaxing in between the cycles. You can feel the blood in your veins and tingling on your skin. Your mind is completely still. There's nothing quite like it.

TEN STEPS TO BADA BASTU LIKE A SWEDE

1. Clear your schedule so you don't need to rush the process.
2. Pack the right gear. Usually bathing suits are banned, but you will need something to sit on and a towel.
3. If the ground is cold, take surf shoes or wool socks.
4. Select the sauna bench carefully; a sauna features a series of benches at different heights. If you're a rookie, it's better to start on the lowest rung where it's cooler and eventually work your way up to the top rung beside the professionals!
5. If you're with a friend, speak in hushed tones so as to not disturb others (or remain silent if sauna etiquette requires this).
6. Stay in the sauna until you are suitably hot but do not exceed 15 to 20 minutes.
7. Take your dip immediately after exiting the sauna. If you are a novice and the water is very cold, don't submerge your head or leave the ladder!
8. Between cycles, find a spot that's sheltered from the wind, rest, and sip water to allow your body to recover and njut!
9. Repeat the cycle up to three times.
10. Stay rehydrated throughout the day.

The **bare** truth

If you feel self-conscious about your body, the *best* place to go is a Swedish sauna. You'll witness body-confident people of all shapes and sizes. Or as my friend David Brain, a British writer and broadcaster who recently moved to Sweden, puts it: "We are all lumpy and oddly shaped. Some people have hair in places others don't. Some people have broad powerful shoulders and weird feet—and for all people, it simply doesn't matter."

It's a healthy revelation when all we're used to seeing are lithe, toned figures in the media. My friend Leah takes her daughters to the local sauna to "change the script," helping them to see that we're all different and yet have the same "brave bodies, dripping wet from the Baltic Sea." The sauna helps you to love your body for what it is. Leaving less room for worrying about jiggly parts, and more time for njutning.

Tångbad

Not buying the cold-water dip? How about something a little warmer? As I grew up in London, my connection with seaweed was on our visits to the South Coast, where we'd wade through slippery tentacles to swim in the English Channel. Occasionally, my sister Charlie would chase me with great armfuls of it as I ran away as fast as I could. If only I'd known about the wonderful health-giving effects of seaweed, as I do now, I might not have been quite so afraid!

One of my first encounters with a *tångbad* (seaweed bath), was at Torekov Warmbadhus on the shore of the Kattegat Sea. The warm bathhouse was made up of a series of candlelit private bathrooms each containing a roll-top tub filled with warm ocean water and freshly harvested bladderwrack seaweed.

The benefits of seaweed have long been known in Sweden. It's rich in oils, minerals, and alginates that are great for the skin and the warm water opens the pores so your body can absorb it, leaving you with a silky-smooth feel. Seaweed is also known for its anti-allergic and anti-inflammatory activities as well as containing an emollient that helps to protect skin from water loss,[53] leaving it soft and well-nourished.

As I cautiously climbed into the tångbad, I was propelled into the tranquillity of the moment—breathing in the scent of the salty ocean air and experiencing the luxurious feel of the warm soft, oily water on my skin before being scrubbed from head to toe with seaweed. Invigorating, yet soothing, I left feeling like a new (and squeaky clean) person.

Why not bring a handful of seaweed back with you from the coast (if permitted in your area)? If it's safe to eat, you can also use seaweed to embellish recipes, adding a touch of salty goodness that's rich in omega-3. You'll prolong that wonderful feeling of being by the ocean. Alternatively, light candles, play soft music, and add a cup of salt, three tablespoons of olive oil, or chamomile or lavender tea to your bathwater for a relaxing soak.

Take to the water

In most countries, sailing is seen as a sport for the elite. But sailing in Sweden is a pastime for everyone. How so? It all stems back to a 1940s contest devised by the Royal Swedish Sailing Association in which designers were asked to design an inexpensive and practical boat. None really fit the bill, but eventually the designs were pooled together, and the affordable *Nordisk Folkbåt* (Nordic Folkboat—literally "the people's boat") was born.[54]

Combined with inexpensive mooring fees and extensive non-tidal waters, and sailing becomes an accessible Swedish national sport. Come late spring, the boatyards are a hive of activity as sailors prepare their beloved vessels for the summer. As a keen sailor, my usually restless husband finds sailing to be the epitome of njuta. "Cruising the waters on a beautiful day is so relaxing, it's just you and the ocean in solitude and silence," he explains, "and after dark, you can't get cozier than the interior of a boat, with its dark wood paneling and oil lamps. But don't get caught in a storm—or it'll be anything but njuta!"

If you live near the ocean, a lake, or a river, why not find a water sport to njuta from? Slower activities that rely on the elements for power are a perfect way to unwind. Many sailing, canoeing, kayaking, and windsurfing clubs offer beginner courses. And even if the weather isn't on your side, as the adage goes: "A rough day at sea is better than any day in the office."

njuta

at home

Our daily interactions with the immediate world around us have a profound effect on our mood, behavior, and overall well-being. It's something Swedes pay close attention to—creating a simple, stylish home is part of their DNA. And you sense this the moment you walk in the door. Minimalistic, yet warm and inviting, the Swedish home emits a wonderful sense of calm and is a soothing space, promoting health and enhancing the quality of life.

Furthermore, in a country with long, hostile winters and where dining out has traditionally been expensive, Swedes spend a lot of time relaxing and entertaining at home and therefore appreciate the importance of creating a comfortable living space that lends itself to savoring small, positive moments.

A recent U.S.-based survey found 96 percent of homeowners say their home is an important contributor to overall happiness.[55] By putting in the effort and getting the décor right, just like our Swedish friends, you can create the ultimate space in which to unwind, be in the present, and create little pockets of happiness throughout your day.

The cozy home

Mysig is a tricky word to pronounce in English (perhaps the closest phonetically is "moo-sig," although Per would still wince!). Either way, the word derives from *mysa* (to smile, slightly, with contentedness) and is used to describe a cozy situation that affords comfort and warmth.

"Not only can physical spaces look mysig, but it can also be used to imply a cozy feeling in your heart," my friend Helena explains. "A Friday night at home around the TV with family is referred to as *fredagsmys* (cozy Friday) and of course your home can have a mysig feel."

While a home can be practical, comfortable, and aesthetically beautiful, making it mysig makes all the difference to the overall experience—and as with all things allowing you to njuta, it requires a little conscious effort!

So how do the Swedes create a mysig home? Let's start with the basics.

FOUR STEPS FOR CREATING A "FEELING FIRST" HOME

Often people make the mistake of focusing on the aesthetics of a home. But as any Swede will tell you, it's equally important to ensure a home is highly functional and comfortable too. And the best way to do this is to take a "feeling first" approach.

1. Focus on how you would like to feel in each room in your home.
2. Understand what is required to create that right feeling in terms of furniture, color, materials, lighting, et cetera.
3. Listen to and trust your intuition and dare to go with it.
4. Embrace the physical property you already have, including the living space and all your possessions.

A home that taps into the senses

What makes us truly connected to a space? A Swede would ensure, perhaps subconsciously, that a home needs to tap into *all* the senses.

Touch

It's often underestimated just how much the way that something feels can transform your perception of an experience. When you decorate your home, selecting beautifully tactile materials can make a huge difference in how you experience your home.

Swedes are drawn to décor and furniture made from natural materials such as leather, wool, linen, stone, glass, and wood, all of which have a definitive feel beneath the fingertips.

"Going back to the olden days in Sweden, materials came from nature, making them 'free,' which is why we have a strong history of craftsmanship," Tina Lekeberg, a Swedish color and material designer, says. In Sweden, 90 percent of all single-family houses are built from wood,[56] and it's also the flooring of choice.

We are all well versed on the benefits of nature on our well-being (see page 85). And interacting daily with natural materials in our home has the same positive effect on our psyche.

Research by the Natural Resource Institute Finland and Tampere University found that when subjects worked in a room made from wood, they saw lower feelings of negativity and irritability and increased energy.[57] And a Japanese study found that touching wood with the palm increased physiological relaxation more than any other material.[58] It also positively affects the air quality, absorbing moisture and sound.

Furthermore, nothing beats the feeling of wood (and other natural materials), as opposed to synthetic material, against the skin. During a recent renovation at our summer cottage,

Per and I ripped out the dated 1970s plastic laminate flooring to reveal an old pine floor underneath. The wood was nicked and pocked, telling the story of its past life, and the warm wood was a joy to walk on, creaking slightly underfoot—like a living, breathing element. It's transformed the way we experience the room.

When you choose items for your home, opt for natural materials with a tactile finish. Even a simple wooden spoon instead of a plastic version will help to elevate your everyday experience at home and boost feelings of calm and well-being!

Smell

When it comes to the home, the role of scent is often overlooked, but even the most subtle of odors can have a powerful effect on how we feel.

The natural materials and excellent ventilation in Swedish homes help to create a pleasant odor, enhanced by the wonderful smell of foraged foliage, plants, and fresh ingredients bubbling on the stove or bread baking in the oven (see page 45).

When you look at the evidence, which suggests 75 percent of our emotions each day are influenced by smells, with moods enhanced by up to 40 percent from a scent we consider pleasant,[59] the Swedes are onto something. In fact, even the most subtle scent can evoke a memory or transport us to another place and time. A bad odor, on the other hand, will have us running for the hills—or at least make it impossible to relax and savor the moment!

Pick your own blooms

Store-bought flowers are traditionally expensive in Sweden, so many prefer to pick their own from the yard or nearby meadows in the spring and summer. Come winter, when the trees are bare, a scavenged evergreen branch or a fir tree sapling do wonders to bring in the wonderful *doft* (scent) of the season (ensuring, of course, that they are taken in a sustainable way).

While store-bought flowers can spark visual joy, the enjoyment you get from picking flowers to create a bouquet is tenfold. And seeing them in the vase escorts you straight back to the meadow/flowerbed you got them from and the feeling of the warm sun on your arms.

FOUR STEPS FOR FORAGING FLOWERS

1. **Do your research on what flowers are suitable to bring indoors (some perish quickly or might be poisonous for animals and small children).**
2. **Pick flowers first thing in the morning to avoid wilting.**
3. **Choose a selection of flowers in different shapes and sizes as well as contrasting colors to create a more interesting bouquet.**
4. **Branches from other plants such as raspberry bushes help to add a wonderful scent to your bouquet as well as a wild touch.**

HOW TO CREATE YOUR WILD BOUQUET

WHAT YOU NEED

- Your favorite flowers
- Knife
- Vase

STEPS

1. Cut the stems on the diagonal and create a one-inch split from the bottom up the middle of the stem with a knife to help the flowers soak up water.

2. Remove any lower leaves so they don't dip into the water.

3. Cross the first three stems and hold them in your nondominant hand.

4. Add more blooms one by one, twisting the stems as you go to form a spiral effect.

5. Think about where you are going to place your bouquet. If it's going on an end table, it will need to be more of a fan shape, with the flowers facing in the same direction. If you're placing it in the center of the room, it should be like a pyramid to ensure it's aesthetically appealing from all sides.

6. Place longer, pointy flowers higher up in the center of your bouquet and rounder, flatter flowers such as peonies lower down at the front, back, and sides. If you have one "showstopper" of a bloom, make sure it can be clearly seen!

7. Think about contrast—combine delicate and strong, and dark and light for a more interesting bouquet.

8. A vase should be at least one-third the size of the bouquet—it's better to go for a smaller vase than one that's too large. But it must be steady and able to hold the weight of your bouquet.

The urban jungle

The benefits of houseplants have been well documented over the years and include improving concentration, de-stressing the mind, and boosting happiness among the many positives. They are also fantastic air purifiers!

Nurturing plants through watering, spritzing, and feeding is a great way to be present and allow your worries to drain away.

Sound

While we walk around, our ears are working away, subtly taking in the environment around us and changing the way we feel about it. Walk into an echoey room, and you're bound to feel uncomfortable. Enter a space with soft, soothing sounds, and you'll feel instantly calm and relaxed. Many of us live in urban areas, where we're constantly tuned into a "sound salad" of traffic, machinery, trains, and general city life. As our body works hard to tune out background noise and focus on what's important, it can wear us down, negatively impacting our well-being without us even realizing it.

Of course, Sweden has several large cities that are no less noisy than other cities. But step inside a home and you are greeted with a wonderful wall of silence. Often blessed with triple- or even quadruple-glazed windows, the sound from outside is buffered. Natural materials like wood and wool help to absorb sound, and layers of textiles in the form of rugs, curtains, cushions, and blankets also help to create a calm oasis in which to relax and be present.

Swapping out your windows is of course a drastic measure, not to mention costly, but there are other ways to dampen the noise. Layer your home with textiles as well as feel-good items like plants and books to absorb sound and create a quieter, calmer space a world away from the bustling streets below.

Sight

One of the first things that drew me to the Swedish home is how aesthetically pleasing they are. Swedes are adept at working with natural and electrical light, filling their home with furniture that combines form and function and drawing on natural surroundings to create a harmonious feel.

See the light

One of the most essential elements in a home is light. Not only does harnessing natural light save electricity, crucially, it makes us feel good. A U.S.-based study found 70 percent of homeowners who have access to natural light at home say it contributes to well-being and 90 percent felt views of the outdoors are an important factor in making a home a happier place to be.[60]

Swedes enjoy an abundance of light in the summertime, but come winter, the darkness sets in. What little natural light filters through is to be highly prized. Heavy, lined curtains are shunned in favor of sheer ones, allowing the soft light to filter through. And furniture is artfully arranged by the windows so residents can take in the great outdoors or simply enjoy life on the street below.

This inadvertently gets the thumbs-up from our brain as natural light stimulates the hormone serotonin, which boosts our mood and helps us to feel calm and in the moment.

A seat by the window

Evolutionarily, we'd feel safer if we had a good vantage point of approaching enemies. It's so ingrained in our psyche today that a spot by the window and/or door of the room is said to make us feel more comfortable, relaxed, and secure.

Satisfying this need doesn't need to be complicated. An armchair or chaise lounge by the window will serve as a cozy spot in which to enjoy your morning coffee, get some light therapy, and chase away the winter blues.

Swedes also love a window seat. It might be as simple as placing a single cushion on a wide windowsill or an all-encompassing built-in wall-to-wall seating and storage solution! Either way, creating a window seat makes a perfect perch from which to watch the shifting nature and the world go by outside—pure meditation!

The **gossi**p mirror

Wander around an old town in Sweden and you'll likely spot what looks like a rearview mirror on the outside of a window frame. Known as a *skvallerspegel*, gossip mirrors were introduced in the eighteenth and early nineteenth century and allow occupants to keep an eye on what's happening in the street without peering out. Crafty!

Ponder the twilight

As the light starts to fade, the world goes through a multitude of magnificent hues including pinks, oranges, and fiery reds. In our busy lives, it's the time of day that so easily passes us by—and yet there is so much enjoyment that can be gleaned from pausing to take in the sunset.

Kura skymning (to sit quietly pondering dusk) is an age-old Swedish tradition that derives from a time before electricity when Swedish families would gather around the fireplace after sunset, tell stories, and snuggle up before the dark set in. In Sweden, far from the equator, twilight can last up to an hour, and in centuries past would signify that it was time for bed. It was nature's way of helping us wind down.

More recently, twilight became a cue for farmers to return home and relax by the fire before evening chores began. Traditionally, it made sense to make the most of every drop of natural light to save money on candles and electricity. And at the same time, it afforded a cherished moment to sit quietly and reflect before dark. Today, the practice has largely gone out of favor, and kura skymning is a little-known ritual except within literary circles, where adult storytelling sessions are still organized at dusk.

Being able to reach for a light switch is a great privilege and something we so often take for granted (until there's a power outage!), but there's something wonderful to be said for being in tune with the fading light. It's arguably the most beautiful time of day. Known as "the golden hour" in photography, it's a time when light scatters over the earth, often erupting in beautiful sunsets that paint the world in an array of reds and pinks—so often missed as we rush about in our stressed-out world.

Instead of reaching for the light switch, why not take a moment to sit quietly and njut from twilight occasionally? It's the perfect opportunity for a break, and if with others, to share your positive experiences from the day or forthcoming plans that will amplify your own positive emotions.[61]

FOUR STEPS FOR LIGHTING UP YOUR HOME

Lighting plays a crucial role in the home and, if done correctly, can make all the difference in creating a comfortable, relaxing living space in which to *trivas* (thrive). After all, it's hard to njuta with a book if you have to strain to see the words. Likewise eating dinner is not so relaxing under the blinding glare of a bare, mega-watt light bulb!

Dimmable lights and candles are two essentials in the Swedish home, transforming a space into a cozy and warm womb-like feel. Here's how to light up your home like a Swede, for the ultimate njutningen:

1. **Consider how you use the space and ensure there is lighting for all the tasks in a room.**

2. **Place lighting at different heights: overhead, on the wall, and on the floor to create interest and ambience.**

3. **Use dimmers so you can adapt lighting according to your needs, the time of day, and your mood.**

4. **Use lighting to highlight the things you love most in your home, including paintings, favorite possessions, and architectural features so you can njuta more from them!**

A beacon in the window

Walk around a European village at night and the closed shutters and curtains give streets a foreboding and deserted feel. Swedes, however, have a tradition of placing lamps with soft low lighting in the window, pooling the lanes with a lovely, warm, and welcoming glow.

From inside, lamps help to compensate for the lack of natural light, making the black rectangle of the window feel less foreboding. Security, coziness, warmth, and welcomeness—perhaps we should all have a lamp in our window.

Candles

You won't find a single Swedish home without a stash of tealights, pillar candles, tapered candles, and oil lamps. *Levande ljus* (live candles) are a staple, and you'll likely witness naked flames on every surface in every room throughout the Swedish home, even in the downstairs bathroom!

"Lighting a candle is a ritual that says the work is done and now it's time to njuta," Per explains. It only takes a second to light a wick, and yet it can make all the difference to a room. Warm, soothing, and relaxing, a naked flame has a meditative effect and emits a wonderful golden glow, drawing you into the present as you bathe in the coziness and warmth of it all.

Always keep a room well-ventilated, keep naked flames away from anything flammable, and never leave a lit candle unattended.

Elevate the home for each season

In my early twenties, I spent a year in Dubai, a part of the world blessed with year-round sunshine and balmy temperatures. It felt like I was permanently on holiday, and I loved it. But after a year, I started to miss the seasons. Where were the falling leaves, the grass blanketed in frost, and the spring flowers?

Given its northern latitude, Sweden has incredibly pronounced seasons, and Swedes are highly tuned to every shift. It's a world of contrast, with an everchanging landscape, from the beautiful summers, with wildflowers dancing in the meadows under the midnight sun, to autumn, where the leaves fall from the trees in a golden spectacle. And then comes the stillness and long shadow of winter, a world blanketed in snow. And finally, the first snowdrops break through the thawing soil, wildflowers appear like stars, and great flocks of birds return from their migration south. Spring has arrived!

In a restless, fast-paced world where everything feels at our fingertips, the slow rhythm of the seasons can be reassuring and grounding, with each new shift proffering a great opportunity to let go of the old and embrace the new.

"In Sweden, we need to embrace each season and make the most of what it has to offer," my friend Maria tells me. "The weather is so changeable and varied. We have learned to seize each opportunity as it arises and live each season intensely so that when it's over, we're ready to move on. In the summer we spend as much time as possible outdoors: eating, swimming, soaking up the sun, and dining alfresco. By the time autumn arrives, we're ready to relax and cozy-up indoors."

In Sweden, it's not just the wardrobe that changes with the season; homes are also adapted to ensure they perfectly match the mood and provide ultimate comfort and relaxation. "We are very in tune with nature and adapting our homes to each season is born out of necessity, but it truly helps us to embrace each and every phase," my friend Malin explains.

In warmer months of the year, the Swedish home takes on an airy feel with lighter textiles including fresh linens and cotton. In winter, the home becomes a cozy cocoon of wool, knits, and sheepskin. Color also plays an important role.

"In Swedish summer cottages, you'll see cooler colors such as blue and white, which reflect the sparkling ocean. In the winter we like to bring in a lot of candles and add warm shades such as red, burgundy, and dark green and brown—it is a time for creating 'visual' warmth to our homes to compensate for the cold outside. It's our way to ensure we feel good at home in each season," my friend, an interior designer, Jannice explains.

Spruce up the home for spring

Spring is a time for new beginnings—and the home is no different. Thick textiles are swapped for fresh linen and cotton, while tulips, hyacinths, and daffodils replace heavier foliage like pine and boxwood. Light colors appear on sofas and beds as well as in the closet. A spring clean is in order, hearths are swept, shelves are dusted, and windows are thrown open to let in the wonderful spring air. Here are some tips for getting into the spring cleaning spirit.

The first step is to declutter and store away winter items. This will create space for your spring and summer belongings.

Next, it is time to give your home a thorough clean. The returning light will reveal cobwebs, settled dust, and marks on windows so a deep clean is necessary.

Use your renewed energy to give rooms a fresh coat of paint and fix any imperfections for a practical, fully functional home fit for a Swede!

It's also important to swap out heavier textiles for lighter linen and cotton. This will give your home a fresh look and help keep you cool during the warmer months. You might also like to move your furniture around to make the most of the returning light. This will help to create a more comfortable and inviting living space.

Finally, it's time to unpack your spring/summer clothes and display your favorite pieces. A flowery dress or a brightly colored shirt can instantly lift the vibe of the room and bring a smile to your face.

Open up your home for summer

Sweden comes alive in the summertime, and life moves outdoors to soak up the abundance of sunshine. Windows are thrown open to fill the home with light and fresh air while light-colored, breathable textiles ensure a cool yet cozy living space and freshly plucked blooms (see page 130) fill the home with the wonderful, sweet scent of summer. Soft blankets and lanterns help to keep the cold at bay after sunset and extend evenings alfresco on balconies or in the backyard.

Entertaining? Do like the Swedes and keep a basket of blankets at the ready to ensure there is one for every guest. Place summery items like sun hats and baskets on display to ensure that the summer season vibe is ever present and dot your home with fresh flowers. There's nothing like the scent of a single rose in the bathroom!

Reset the home for autumn

As the temperatures lower, it's natural to gravitate indoors. Do as the Swedes and ready your home for the *mysiga* (cozy) season ahead. Think layers of thick, soft natural textures in the form of blankets, cushions, and rugs. And don't forget to head out to the woods to pick up pine cones and other beautiful foliage before displaying them in bowls around your home to draw the season indoors.

Cozy up your home come winter

There's something wonderful about a Swedish home in the wintertime. The warm glow of lights, the flicker of a candle, and a lantern by the front door guiding you home—it's like a welcoming hug. Do like the Swedes and don't be afraid to light candles at breakfast, lunch, and supper, while you read, or while you soak in the tub. Getting the lighting just right is also a wonderful way to elevate your mood. Dimmers and low-level mood lighting do wonders to create a warm and relaxing feel.

Don't stop there, though. Do as our Scandi friends and scatter blankets, throws, and sheepskins throughout your living space. Combine plenty of natural materials like wool, stone, and leather, and nature will never feel far away.

Think about your home and its surroundings—how can you draw each season indoors using colors, textiles, and even furnishings? Suss out each room and the feeling you're looking to create and choose colors associated with this. It doesn't have to be on the walls, ceiling, or floors; it could also be in the form of accessories such as cushions, vases, or candles. Likewise, at the end of each season, re-evaluate your home like you would your wardrobe, storing away more wintery items. You'll appreciate what you have even more if you don't see it for a while!

Color therapy

You might think of a Swedish home as white, white, and um, more white. But these days, that's not the case. Muted, earthy, natural shades are used to elevate the home and mirror the surroundings for greater harmony. And painting is a great budget-friendly way to elevate your living space.

"When I moved into my new apartment after my divorce, I had a tight budget with which to decorate," Tina recalls.

"Paint is inexpensive, and I knew that if I could get the colors just right, I would create a beautiful, personal living space in which to relax."

THREE SHADES THAT HELP ADD HARMONY TO A HOME, SWEDISH STYLE

1. **WHITE** Fresh, pure, and serene, white helps to lighten up a space—especially in low-light conditions. It's also very calming. A study on color preferences found adults ranked white number one for evoking moods of quietness and concentration[62]—an important feeling if you're looking to njuta! Be wary though: "White is a very bright and intense color. Swedes tend to blend in gray or beige tones to soften it up and add warmth," advises Tina.

2. **EARTHY GREEN** Commonly perceived as reassuring, warm, and settling, earthy tones are an ideal way to create a calming atmosphere at home. Soft green is a popular shade in Swedish country homes since it helps to connect the living space to the woods and open landscapes. It's also said to have a restorative quality, helping to soothe and calm the mind.

3. **BLUE** This is a popular choice in Swedish coastal homes and in the bedroom since it represents the ocean and sky. Go for a soft, earthy medium-blue with gray undertones to help lower your pulse, clear the mind, and restore calm.

Good design makes you happy

"Pleasure in a thing of beauty is the essence of a happy life."

—Zino Davidoff, entrepreneur

From soothing minimalist interiors to handicrafts and iconic furniture, good design is everywhere in Sweden—and it makes a huge impact on how we feel.

Think back to your last visit to a fast-food joint. You likely sat on plastic seating under fluorescent lights and all you wanted to do was eat and go—am I right? Places like that don't want you to hang around and njuta, so they design the environment to emphasize the "fast food" concept! Compare this to a cozy, candlelit restaurant with gentle music and soft, upholstered chairs. The mood set is to make you feel warm and relaxed and like you are somewhere you'd like to linger and savor the food and the experience.

While we can't control all environments, we can control the immediate environment in our home. And the furniture we choose is crucial to how much we can njuta!

Swedes go to great lengths to fill their homes with well-designed objects that not only look good but are functional too. For good reason: a study commissioned by the HTC Corporation discovered that surrounding yourself with well-designed objects that combine form and function triggers feelings of calm and contentment and reduces negative emotions such as anger and annoyance by nearly a third (29 percent)! At the same time, items that are designed purely for function but are not pleasing to the eye triggered negative emotions such as gloominess and depression by an alarming 23 percent.[63]

Looking for greater njutning at home? Here's what to look for:

Furniture that's built to last

Given that Swedes enjoy a great work-life balance and tend to socialize more at home than out, they spend a lot of time indoors. Especially in winter. This means that furniture gets a lot more wear and tear.

"Swedish design classics are crafted with the idea that you are going to spend a lot of time in them," interior designer Bettina explains. "You come home from work, rest, and recuperate, so furniture needs to be both comfortable and durable."

Indeed, many Swedish design classics don't *look* comfortable at first sight thanks to their slim, minimalist form. But once you recline in a Lamino or Pernilla easy chair, you won't want to get up. Ergonomically designed to follow the contours of your body, Swedish design classics are supremely comfortable. And, of course, they're a dream to look at. But they can be costly. Learning from the generations before, however, many Swedes understand the value of saving up and investing in good design.

"Iconic pieces are often more of an investment, but if you're going to spend money on your home, buying a classic is a safe bet," my friend Ullis explains. "We strive to be resourceful and think sustainably. Trends come and go, but an iconic piece will never go out of fashion. They're timeless and you'll never tire of them—they're a part of our heritage and something you will always njuta from."

In our throw-away culture, everything you could need is within reach. But is it well made? Will it stand the test of time? What might be considered "cheap" now could be very costly if you have to replace it in a few years' time. Longing for an item for your home and saving up your pennies to buy it will not only mean you'll appreciate it more when you buy it, but if it's well made, you can appreciate it for years to come and pass it on to the next generation too!

FIVE ICONIC SWEDISH DESIGN PIECES TO NJUTA IN

1. **EVA LOUNGE CHAIR** Recognized by its organically curved backrest, comfy armrest, and solid wood legs, the Eva Lounge Chair was designed by Kerstin H. Holmquist in 1958 and has been a comfortable favorite for more than sixty years.

2. **A2 ARMCHAIR** Furniture designer Arthur Lindqvist gained recognition in 1930 for his coveted outdoor chair with its wood seat and spring steel construction, allowing you to peacefully rock while listening to birdsong.

3. **PERNILLA 69 EASY CHAIR** Swedish furniture designer and architect Bruno Mathsson experimented with snow imprints from his body, which he used to create furniture that follows the human form. Made from molded and layered beech wood, the Pernilla 69 easy chair is supremely comfortable. Add a footrest and a blanket for ultimate njutning.

4. **LAMINO CHAIR** Designed in 1956 by Yngve Ekström, the timeless and popular Lamino Chair follows the human form, making it a supremely pleasant place to relax! I particularly love the sheepskin option for added warmth and softness!

5. **JETSON MATSEN ARMCHAIR** This iconic easy chair designed by Bruno Mathsson reflects his passion for comfort combined with a Swedish design approach. The bowl-shaped seat, ergonomic back, head cushion, and swivel base will mean you'll never want to get up!

Elevate your home with all-important extras

My friend Malin has the loveliest home. Not only does it look wonderful, but it also *feels* wonderful. What's her secret? "I had njutning at the forefront of my mind when I planned my home," she explained over a fika (see page 57). "It was important to me that every room contained thoughtful touches so that my family and I can relax and be in the moment."

The key is to go that extra mile and enhance each room with small touches to subtly elevate everyday experiences. It might be a chair in the bathroom so you can sit and apply your moisturizer in comfort, a soft blanket waiting to be unfurled on the sofa, or two fluffy single duvets instead of a double, so you can have just the thickness you desire for a cozy night's slumber.

With a little thought and effort, you'll have a truly mindful home with small moments of pleasure waiting around every corner.

Follow your heart

One of the stand-out factors of the Swedish Gen Z home? A *fulsnygg* piece. Literally meaning "ugly pretty," the word is usually used for a person who isn't conventionally beautiful but attractive in their own way. But I think it fits well with home décor too.

In the home, we tend to play it safe and fear judgment from visitors. But instead of following the trends and second-guessing what others might think, if you really want to create a home to njuta from, it's important to follow your heart.

Fill your living space with inherited items that tell a story of your family's past with vintage and flea market finds—furniture you've upcycled yourself, reminders of special heartwarming moments in your life, and other personal possessions.

And the next time you're in a vintage shop and something attracts your attention and puts a smile on your face—like a crazy lamp with a bold oversize print in zesty colors—why not go for it? It's bound to be a great conversation starter with friends too!

A home without distractions, so you can relax

It's easy to assume that the more we have, the happier we'll be, but exercising restraint and adopting a "less is more" philosophy like the Swedes is conducive to greater happiness.

It's hard to njuta from a space that's full of hoards of stuff or so messy you can't see a single clean surface!

But it's nothing that a little Swedish *döstädning* (the Swedish art of death cleaning) can't fix!

Döstädning

"How's your mother?" I asked Per after he had a lengthy phone chat with her a few weeks ago. "She's in the process of döstädning," came the casual response. "That sounds a bit morbid," I replied, slightly shocked.

Döstädning is the process of freeing yourself and your family from a lifetime of clutter, before, um, you kick the bucket.

Let's face it, no one wants to think about their demise. But I'm not surprised that the process exists in Sweden; after all, they're a highly practical bunch and very respectful of others.

"Death cleaning has become popular in Sweden, especially in recent years," Christina tells me. "Cleaning out your home and organizing your estate as well as allocating assets in advance is a great way to ease the burden on your successors and save them the hassle, embarrassment, and any potential squabbles after you've gone!"

Christina might have a point.

When you go, your family has enough to deal with, without clearing out a lifetime of clutter, potentially uncovering cringe-worthy photos, diaries, and other items that may be lurking in your attic.

It may sound like a task for the elderly, but really, why wait? There's something great about being free of unnecessary clutter, and you'll feel highly organized and relaxed afterward. Plus, the process itself can be highly meditative and something you might just njuta from.

The clean home

Many describe my home as "homey" (very likely a synonym for messy!), but I still take it as a compliment! To me, homey means cozy and comfortable—somewhere with soul. But there are limits—it's hard to switch off, relax, and savor the moment if you're surrounded by chaos!

Swedes tend to be highly organized and generally have less stuff. So even if their homes are a little *stökigt* (messy) from time to time, it still gives the illusion of feeling light and airy and, well, *neater*! Which is way more relaxing as a result.

FOUR QUICK TRICKS TO ENJOY A NEATER HOME, SO YOU CAN RELAX

1. **Ensure that there is a place for everything and that everything is in its place.**
2. **Make it easy for children to keep things picked up by using big storage containers so they can throw stuff in them.**
3. **"Reset" your home every now and then by setting a timer for twenty minutes and getting everyone on board for a fast and furious cleanup!**
4. **Don't beat yourself up. Sometimes something must give—remember that others don't "see" your mess as much as you do!**

Appreciate what you have, over and over again

One of the beautiful things about a Swedish home is how they display their possessions. My friend Tina likens it to still life. Why not channel the Swedes and be a curator of your space? Look at display areas such as shelves and end tables as a canvas on which to paint—and take time to group your knickknacks into new and interesting combinations to create interest and spark joy. Play with height, shape, and contrast with groupings of three, five, or seven items, leaving blank spaces between the groups. Update the displays regularly for a new take on old pieces.

Not only will you enjoy the creative process, but you'll also see your possessions in a whole new way and njuta from them all over again.

Create a window garden

Plants are great for relieving stress and boosting our mood. If you live in an urban environment (or a place like Sweden where the trees lose their leaves for six months of the year), try placing lots of plants on or around your windowsill. It's a popular tactic used by our Nordic friends, giving the illusion that there's greenery outside, even in winter!

Add botanical prints

Scroll through Swedish country homes on Instagram and you'll discover a surprising touch—wallpaper, upholstery, cushions, and porcelain with bold botanical patterns! This trend links back to Sweden's strong arts and crafts heritage and offers a great way to draw nature indoors. When you consider that just looking at a landscape painting can help to reduce stress and fatigue by up to 40 percent,[64] this is a great way to create a more mindful, feel-good space in which to njuta naturally!

THREE POPULAR SWEDISH DESIGN PATTERNS INSPIRED BY NATURE

1. **PERSONS KRYDDSKÅP** Designed in 1955 by textile designer Astrid Sempe, this kitchen herb motif has become a well-loved classic in Swedish kitchens.

2. **TULPANER** Josef Frank's colorful nature-inspired patterns for Svenskt Tenn add comfort and a homey feel while exuding a sense of freedom. *Tulpaner* (tulips) and others of his botanical designs remain hugely popular today.

3. **BERSÅ** Designed in 1961 by textile artist and illustrator Stig Lindberg, this beloved green leaf pattern remains a staple in Swedish homes.

An outdoor space made for njutning

"Every summer there are a number of nights, not many, but a number, when everything is perfect. The light, the warmth, the smells, the mist, the birdsong—the moths. Who can sleep? Who wants to?"

—Fredrik Sjöberg, writer, *The Fly Trap*

Outdoor spaces are an important part of the Swedish living space—after all, they have to wait a long time for the good weather to arrive, and they're not going to miss it!

Nothing quite beats the feeling of the great outdoors, surrounded by greenery and the scent of the season while birds and insects go about their work.

From sowing and growing your own fruits and vegetables to lush balconies and greenhouses, there is no end to the njutning you can get from your outdoor space, no matter how small.

Dare to fail

I used to be terrible at looking after plants and flowers. But in recent years I've become a little better—some might even say "obsessed" (there's a certain lemon tree . . .). The truth is, it's so unbelievably satisfying and rewarding to nurture plants from seed.

Having said that, gardening can be a tricky business, and you're bound to fail from time to time. To get enjoyment from it, it's important to ease the pressure of success—the prizewinning zucchinis can wait! It's the planning, toiling, sowing, watering, and pruning that's known to calm the mind, soothe negative emotions, put us in the here and now, and boost our ability to focus on the positive.

Swedes are careful not to "overdo" their yards and take a "less is more" approach to avoid too much gardening and not enough njutning!

If done right, you too can create an outdoor space in which to relax, focus on your surroundings, and connect with nature, surrounded by the beauty of all your favorite blooms!

FIVE ELEMENTS FOR A CALM AND RELAXED YARD

1. **PLANT A TREE** They provide shelter, shade, and if you're lucky, delicious fruit. Evolutionarily, they also serve as a lookout tower and a place to hide from enemies—one of the reasons trees make us feel calm today.

2. **THE SOUND OF WATER** Clean, fresh, babbling water has always been key to our survival. These days, even the sight and sound of water have a soothing effect.

3. **GET RID OF OVERGROWTH** While planting things is great for the environment, too many undesirable weeds such as stinging nettles and brambles can make us feel uneasy! Evolutionarily, this type of growth was hard (and painful) to navigate, and we still feel the anxious effects of this today.

4. **A PATHWAY** Psychologically, we feel so much calmer if we can see a clear exit. Make sure you include a path of some sort through your blooms!

5. **PLANT NATIVE FLOWERS AND PLANTS** If you do so, your yard is more likely to flourish and will become a wonderful environment for local creatures great and small! Do some research to find out about native species in your area and create a yard that will also help wildlife thrive.

Njuta in the garden

While gardening can be therapeutic, the real njutning comes when your work is done, and you can finally put down your trowel, sit back, and relax! Just as a Swede would carve out individual zones in an open-plan room, the yard too contains several "zones" to ensure maximum me time!

Follow the sun

"A life without love is like a year without summer."

—Swedish proverb

Swedes are like flowers; if the sun is out, so are they! And who can blame them? In my view, there's nothing more wonderful than feeling the warm sun on your skin and soaking up all the wonderful light—especially when you haven't seen it for a while. It's so simple yet so incredibly relaxing.

While in some countries the relaxation areas in the yard are designed around shade, in Sweden they follow the sun. And this means having multiple sites, for the best possible vantage points depending on the weather and time of day!

Christina, has a table and chair at the foot of her garden for her morning coffee, an arrangement in the shade of the cottage at the back for when the heat has become too much or there's an easterly wind, and furniture on the terrace for late-afternoon and evening sun. This sounds like she owns some kind of luxury estate, but this is certainly not the case. Christina simply makes the most of the space she has and is one of the most understated people I know. Pretty much all her outdoor furniture is secondhand and simply rests on the grass. But she's ensured all bases are covered for maximum njutning depending on her mood, the time of day, and the weather!

Think about how you use your garden at different times of the day and create zones to ensure that everything is in place—easy chairs, large loungers, and comfortable outdoor dining furniture all guarantee you'll feel relaxed and in the moment. Oh, and keep cushions, extra blankets, and candles on hand for a warm and cozy atmosphere after dark!

Indoor-outdoor feel

The weather is somewhat unpredictable in Sweden (it's been known to snow in midsummer!). Swedes, therefore, become creative in finding ways in which they can relax and enjoy the warmth of the sun's rays while sheltered from the elements! Arbors, annexes, and conservatories are all popular. But there's one garden structure that's really come into its own in recent years: *the greenhouse*!

Traditionally used for *odling* (cultivating plants and flowers), our Nordic friends have caught onto their worth as a perfect sunroom. Naturally warm thanks to the glass, and creating a wonderful sensation of sitting outside, a greenhouse is a perfect place to sip coffee, read a book, take a nap, and enjoy dinners *almost* alfresco.

Why not repurpose the outdoor structures you have in your yard? With a little creativity and effort, they might just become your favorite place to relax!

The outdoor kitchen

Or why not go a step further? *Utekök* (outdoor kitchens) are becoming increasingly popular in Sweden—after all, when the good weather finally arrives, they don't want to miss a second—and cooking everything alfresco is a popular pastime.

As with all things Swedish, it's a case of less is more: a gas stove, access to water (potentially a tank with a faucet that you can fill up manually), shelving for pots, pans, plates, dishes, and utensils, and some fresh herbs, as well as shelter from the wind and rain, is basically everything you might need to enjoy cooking in the great outdoors without having to go back and forth to the kitchen.

The practical basket

Don't have an outdoor kitchen? The idea of carrying plates, glasses, accessories, and food back and forth from the kitchen to the garden can be enough of a deterrent to skip alfresco dining altogether. Practical Swedes often use a traditional hard wicker basket with a handle that holds everything, and it's easy to carry too, so everything gets to its destination in one piece!

After dark

As the summer sun lowers in the sky, the Swedish outdoor space is filled with lanterns, string lights, and blankets (as well as mosquito nets!) for a mysig (cozy) evening under the stars. But there's one element that Swedes enjoy all year round—maybe even more in winter. A firepit! After all, there's nothing like a brasa (fire) to generate warmth and togetherness.

During the pandemic, a firepit was probably built every second in yards across the U.K.! And, of course, they're extremely popular among Swedes too, especially in the wintertime. In the cold and dark of winter, warm clothing is crucial because if you stand still long enough, you'll start to feel the chill.

Who doesn't love a hot chocolate and marshmallows around a fire? You might even like to roast sausages or make pinnbröd (bread twisted around a stick and grilled over a fire) (see page 101).

Looking to build a firepit in your yard? Do like the Swedes and keep it simple. After all, the idea is to feel like you're in the wild and reconnect with nature. Plus, they're quick to build and affordable if you build one yourself.

HOW TO MAKE A FIREPIT

WHAT YOU NEED

- Shovel
- Bucket of water
- Sand
- Bricks or stones to line the edge of the pit
- Wood and kindling
- Matches
- Cushions and blankets

STEPS

1. Pick a spot far from structures, trees, and flammable items (observe local health and safety laws and regulations).
2. Make sure you have easy access to water.
3. Dig a hole according to the width you would like (in accordance with local laws).
4. Line the hole with sand.
5. Place bricks or stones around the edge of the hole.
6. Place seating around the edge (wood logs will do)—if cold, do as a Swede and place a seat pad (see page 97), sheepskin, or reindeer skins over the logs for comfort.

The raised firepit

While barbecues are popular the world over, they're usually tended to by one person and maybe another for company! In the north, Swedes have taken things up a notch with a tripod firepit. Not only can you either grill or attach a cauldron, but the tripod also means everyone can gather around, with their feet tucked under for extra warmth— furthermore, the smoke heads up into the stars rather than your eyes! An all-around winner!

Always observe local laws about outdoor fires. Never leave a fire unattended and always extinguish the fire once you have finished with it.

njuta

at work

Arbetsglädje **is a word** the Swedes use to describe an overall feeling of work-related joy or to experience inner well-being and peace of mind at work. I assure you that it's possible, even though njuta is not a word Swedes usually associate with work! In fact, quite the opposite; it's knowing your hard work is done and the *disconnection* from it that allows one to njuta.

But when you consider that the standard work hours of countries around the world are around forty to forty-four hours per week (with a huge variation around the world), it's important to consciously carve out small moments during your workday to press the pause button and experience a little arbetsglädje and njutning!

It all starts with your morning

If your alarm rings at an ungodly hour and you're constantly just barely keeping up, you're bound to dread weekday mornings. But what happens if you turn the morning around and prep the night before? Set your alarm a little earlier, and sit down and enjoy your first coffee of the day in *lugn och ro* (peace and quiet)—or better still, take a morning dip (see page 113). Not only will you not dread your mornings so much, but you'll also get off on the right foot and set a positive path for the rest of the day.

Change things up every now and then

We are creatures of habit, choosing to eat the same food, read the same kinds of books, and sit in the same chair day in and day out. What happens if you shake things up a little? Small changes in your routine can do wonders to shift your perspective on life and appreciate the world around you. Try a new style of breakfast, switch to a different the radio station, or say *ja!* (yes!) to something you'd ordinarily say no to.

It's easy to get stuck in the rut of rushing to work—same route, same form of transportation. But it's when you shake things up a little that the magic happens. Change your usual route and you'll discover new scenery, see new faces, and pass exciting establishments you might not have seen before. Swapping your car or the train for a bike (see page 60) is also a great way to get out of "robot" mode and into the moment!

"I usually turn right out of my house to get to work in the fastest way," my neighbor Matts Elmenius muses. "But recently I decided to turn left and take a slower route that runs along the coast. It's transformed my commute and makes a huge difference to my journey and the way I view it!"

Start by making one small change today. It's a simple yet great way to snap out of autopilot and into the present and be more in tune with your surroundings.

Plan a little njutning

Feel the Monday blues? Plan something to look forward to during your workday. Just knowing you have a coffee break with a fun colleague, or that you'll be stepping out to buy a piece of cake from your favorite bakery, might just give you the boost you need and ensure you njuter a little from your day.

The work environment

Having read chapter 6, you have no doubt made your home a calm oasis full of cozy corners designed for quiet contemplation or a good book! But what about your workspace?

I know the workspace can look very different depending on your career, and many of us have little or no autonomy over it. But there might just be tiny things you can change to ensure you *trivs* (thrive) and experience a little njutning here and there.

"I aim to get some form of njutning from all the physical spaces in my life, and this includes my office," my friend Sofie, a school social worker, tells me. "If I'm in an environment where I can access small emotional rewards, I am more sensitive and tolerant of others."

Sofie has gone to great lengths to transform her office, even exchanging the standard school curtains for beautiful, sheer linen drapes. This might be a step too far in most workplaces, but there are a few small things you can do to boost your daily experiences and njuta from your environment.

Plug in Bring headphones to tune out background noise and listen to the music you love. For creativity, hit the play button on classical music; for something calm, the sound of nature does wonders. Either way, soothing sounds are a great way to block out the "noise" (see page 133) and give your day a lift.

Surround yourself with pictures of people and places you love You can even include your next vacation destination to remind you why you are working. The pictures will fire off feel-good endorphins, giving you micro-moments of njuta!

Add physical memorabilia They say an organized desk is an organized mind, so it's best not to add clutter! But one or two small, meaningful items can go a long way to remind you of a special person, place, or moment in your life. "On my desk, I have a paperweight my son gave me and a seashell given to me by someone who wanted to remind me to take a break," says Sofie. "They are tiny reminders to take my foot off the pedal for a moment." A 2005 study showed that two ten-minute sessions per day over the span of a week to reminisce about a positive event showed an increased positive effect on our psyche.[65]

Make yourself comfortable An ergonomic workspace is tantamount to health. But to really njuta, you need to go that extra mile. Do you have a workspace where it can get a little cold with the AC? Keep a soft blanket or a nice sweater on hand and your favorite, divine-smelling lotions to moisturize the hands!

Add plenty of plants Greenery is a workspace's best friend. Aside from the numerous health benefits (see page 132), it can also act as a screen for privacy and dampen sound, so you'll feel more comfortable and relaxed!

Re-energize throughout the day

You can't sit at your desk for eight hours straight and be effective. No one can. To take a lunch break away from your desk is a must, but how about other times of the day when your energy wanes?

Research has shown taking a break helps to reduce stress and boost productivity, and Swedes are way ahead of the game on this, taking multiple guilt-free fika paus (coffee and cake away from your work) throughout the day.

"Generally, you get to know your colleagues better in Sweden, and I think that's because of the fika breaks," my friend Bettina, who has worked in finance in Sweden, London, and Luxemburg, tells me. "Fika is a time to talk about life outside of work and even the bosses join. Everyone is considered to be on the same level."

Stopping and doing something for *you*—whether that's going for a coffee, soaking up the sun for ten minutes, or reading the paper—helps to restore your energy and makes you more efficient when you return. So go ahead and take those breaks, and njut.

Feel challenged

"Better to listen to a broken string than never having bent a bow."

—Swedish proverb

Challenges in the workplace come in all shapes and forms: a big project, problem-solving, or overcoming something out of your comfort zone, like presenting in front of an audience or learning a new skill. "For me, work is not about prestige or proving myself to others, it's about whether I am learning something new—it should be a journey," my friend Maria Gustavsson tells me. "I strive to constantly grow as a person and have fun at work. I love to feel energized and have a job where I continue to feel curious."

Stepping out of your comfort zone, challenging yourself to try something new, and developing and honing your skills helps you to grow as a person as well as boost your sense of satisfaction—but best of all, once the hard work is done, you'll truly njuta from the results!

Njuta from the moment

When you're in the thick of things, it's so easy to get side-tracked and look at what lies ahead or reflect on incidents from the past. But forcing your mind to be in the present puts you in a position of power and helps to calm the mind.

While driving through Sweden last summer, I was listening to Swedish World Cup alpine ski racer Sara Hector reflect on her career on *Sommarprat* (summer talk), a popular radio series in which well-known Swedes talk about their lives.

Sara talked through the highs and lows of her career, building up to the moment she won her first gold medal at the Beijing Winter Olympics in 2022.

Finding herself in potential medal contention, Sara was crippled with nerves before her final run and had been unable to eat or sleep. But high up on the mountain right before her descent, she had a moment of clarity and did something she had never done before. She stopped to savor the moment. She thought about how after years of training and hard work, she was finally here, skiing in the Olympics, and with a chance of a medal no less! She took in the scenery, the beautiful day, the crowds cheering below her. And she felt a sense of calm.

Moments later she skied down to claim Olympic gold.

Compare this to a guy I met at a party recently. "When do you njuta most?" I quizzed. He looked at me with a forlorn expression before explaining he'd spent twenty years setting up and growing a start-up, which had been a huge success, and he was about to sell it and retire. "The sad thing is, I've been so focused on the result and thinking I could relax once the work was done that I have lost myself in the process. Do I feel excited about the windfall? Not especially! I see now, I should have taken my time to enjoy the journey and appreciate the small moments along the way."

When working toward a project or goal, direct your attention to what's happening now and what you can control while savoring the small moments along the way. Success is bound to follow . . . and even if it doesn't, you've enjoyed the process anyway!

Celebrate your achievements

So often we rush straight on to the next thing without so much as a backward glance. But just as we should consciously enjoy a "pinch me" moment while in the thick of things, it's even more important to njuta from completed goals and successes—no matter how tiny! Do as the Swedes and have a slice of *tårta* (cake) and revel in the moment!

Redefine success

"Money opens all gates but heaven's."
—Swedish proverb

A "successful" person has long been defined as someone who has made a lot of money. Maybe they have a house with a pool and a tennis court or travel the world. But living in Sweden has taught me to think differently about what success *really* is. Being a humble society, it's frowned upon to be lavish and frivolous with money. Instead, the focus is on working toward the collective good of everyone.

"Really, success is how much you can *njuta av livet* (savor moments in life)," Bettina tells me wisely. "I generally think the Swedish heritage is to take the opportunity to relax and enjoy yourself rather than how much money you have in the bank. You focus on what you have rather than what you don't have. It's a much healthier outlook on life." Wise words indeed!

> Feeling poor? Focus your mind on all the little things in your life that you feel gratitude for. It will help you to focus on the positive aspects of your life, and although you might not have amassed a fortune, you might just feel richer than ever.

Quiet quitting

The hashtag #quietquitting has been viewed more than 159 million times on TikTok. The phrase refers to doing the bare minimum at work, without going above or beyond the tasks you've been assigned or staying beyond a minute longer than needed. It's causing quite a stir in the business world—not to mention panic among employers. In Sweden, not so much.

In some countries around the world, it's considered prestigious to work late, and seen as "hardworking" and "dedicated." In Sweden, it's the opposite. "Swedes have a long history of distancing themselves from stress," trend expert Stefan Nilsson explains. "We love to use phrases such as 'better a little dirt in the corners than clean hell,' recognizing the importance of not overworking something and taking time out to re-energize."

In Sweden, people don't stay at work for an arbitrary amount of time just to impress their managers. Instead, it's about getting the tasks you're assigned done and ensuring a good work-life balance. Stay late, and you'll quickly have your manager on your back, questioning your workload and concerned for your health! You see, Swedes have caught onto the fact that working long hours is not sustainable and is bad for their well-being. And this in turn is bad for business. So get your tasks done to the best of your ability and go home and njut!

Njuta from your vacation

Ask a Swede when they njuter most and the summer vacation will no doubt pop up! Understandable really—I mean, who doesn't enjoy carefree days, kicking back, and relaxing in the sunshine?

All Swedes are entitled to twenty-five full days of annual leave; however, when you consider personal days—for example, at some companies you are entitled to a paid day off to move (*I know!*) and public holidays (known as "red days")—Swedes enjoy up to forty-one paid days off annually. That's an entire two months to do what they like each year!

In the summer, it's not uncommon for Swedes to take three consecutive weeks off (with some taking up to five or even six weeks). And no boss bats an eyelid; they're on vacation too!

Try to send an email in July and you'll get a firm "out of office." Summer is a time for putting down tools, kicking back, and making the most of the good weather.

Compare this to the U.S., where more than half of employees don't take all their paid vacation, and one in four have never taken two consecutive weeks of vacation.[67] When they do clock out, three out of five Americans admit to checking emails and/or making work-related calls due to worry, feeling guilty, and being unable to disconnect from work while on vacation.[68]

It's time to change the narrative. Ensure you take all your annual leave and be firm about setting your "out of office" so you can relax and re-energize. Encourage others to do the same, and never disturb someone on their time off unless it's an emergency. It's hard to relax and savor the moment if you fear a work call at any minute!

The great summer getaway

So where do Swedes go? With more than half of Swedes owning or having access to a summer cottage in the countryside or by the ocean, summer cottages offer Swedes much-needed solitude, a place to disconnect, recharge, and simply be in the moment.

Usually pared-back, fuss-free affairs (some of my friends' cottages don't have electricity or running water and many have an outdoor bathroom!), spending time at a summer cottage is about leading a humble lifestyle. "When you strip your life back to the bare basics and participate in everyday activities like collecting firewood and swimming in the ocean, life slows down and you're entirely in the present—there's a wonderful overall contentment in that," my friend interior designer Helen Sturesson enthuses.

Det blir som det *blir*
(it'll be what it'll be)

For a Swede, with no early mornings and no schedules
to keep, the summer vacation is a simple rhythm of
eat, sleep, swim, repeat while (hopefully) feeling
the warm sun on their skin and the coolness of the
water on their body, and savoring the taste of
smultron (wild strawberries). It's relaxing in
every way—even if the weather gods aren't always
on their side!

Our Nordic friends are on the right track. Taking
annual leave is vital to our long-term mental
health and well-being (people who take vacations
are less likely to feel stressed and suffer from
cardiovascular disease[69] and depression[70]). What
better way to enjoy it than to switch off and njuta
from everything that summer has to offer?

This year set yourself a goal to take all your paid annual leave—you don't need to go anywhere, staycationing and soaking up your immediate surroundings is a fantastic, budget-friendly way to unwind, be in the moment and *återhämter* (recover)! Your employer will thank you, as you'll be more energized and productive when you return!

If you do go away, think about staying somewhere off the grid. There's something wonderful about going offline and getting back to basics—it puts everything into perspective and helps you appreciate the "luxuries" you have once you're home.

Did you know . . . it's not only during your vacation that helps you to njuta; a survey conducted by the Institute for Applied Positive Research found 97 percent of participants say having a trip planned makes them happier and 71 percent responded that they felt greater levels of energy when they had a trip planned in the next six months.[71] A little daydreaming never harmed anyone!

njuta

with friends and family

To really njuta, many Swedes tell me, requires them to disconnect: disconnect from work and disconnect from the people around you. To njuta is a personal moment of contentment between you and your immediate environment, soaking up all the positives of the moment. But to njuta can also be to step back and quietly observe the feeling you get from being around people you love and witnessing their happiness, creating warmth in your heart.

It all starts with a hug

The first time you meet a Swede, a handshake (or these days, maybe an elbow bump) is required. But once you're acquainted, a *kram* (hug) is required. And this warm greeting is something I've grown to appreciate. To be enveloped in someone's arms for a moment gives you a sense of belonging. It makes you feel safe, reassured, calm, relaxed, and like one of the family!

Did you know . . . hugging for longer than 30 seconds increases your level of oxytocin, a chemical in your brain that makes you feel good? Not only that but embraces have health benefits such as reducing blood pressure.[72] So, the next time you hug someone, slow down, be present, and get all the feel-good vibes . . . just not with a Swede you've only just met!

Friendship

A highly guarded bunch, with an immense respect for personal space, it can take years to make friends in Sweden. But it's worth the wait. Once you *do* break into the trusted inner circle you have a friend for life.

The coveted spot comes with a fierce loyalty that makes you feel secure, loved, and appreciated, making it easy to njuta in their company.

"I've known many of my friends since school, and I trust them implicitly," my friend Ullis confides. "In Sweden, we're not really ones for small talk, so I choose my friends wisely, preferring to spend time with people I trust and feel great to be around."

> With all the stresses and strains in life and given how limited our time is, choose your friends wisely, and surround yourself with only people you love, trust, and feel good around while distancing yourself from those who constantly inspire negativity and drama.

Speech is silver, silence is golden

Don't feel like conversing in someone's company? Once all the hugging is over, Swedes are perfectly happy to sit in companionable silence.

I have to say, I found the silences incredibly awkward at first—in the U.K. a break in a conversation is a disaster and something to be filled without fail! Saying anything is better than saying nothing at all! Swedes, on the other hand, shy away from small talk, filling the gaps with simple sighs and audible intakes of breath.

"We're not fans of small talk in Sweden," Per muses. "We'd rather wait until there's something meaningful to say. My friends and I often enjoy companionable silence, which gives me time to think and reflect . . . to njuta."

Feel the love

> "A kiss is a lovely trick designed by nature to stop speech when words become superfluous."
>
> —Ingrid Bergman, actress

Älskar (verb), *kärlek* (noun), *kär* (adjective) . . . there are quite a few words you can use to talk about "love" in the Swedish language. And just like anywhere else in the world, love evokes immense feelings of well-being and happiness.[73] But in my eyes, the Swedish approach to relationships differs somewhat. Swedes favor independence and equality over any form of chivalry, forging an authentic and genuine relationship.

Even so, they do love a *puss* (kiss) just as much as anyone else. And when you consider that locking lips triggers a cocktail of chemicals in your brain that makes you feel euphoric,[74] I wonder if we're puckering up as much as we should?

An important reminder to snatch small moments throughout your day to steal a kiss—a perfect micro-moment to njuta!

189

Four-legged friends

All this chat of family, and I still haven't mentioned man's best friend!

Cats, dogs, hamsters—whatever your preferred type of furry companion, there's no denying the therapy you get from a pet. Our four-legged friends stimulate all the senses: the touch of their fur or skin, their smell, the sound of a purr . . . maybe not always their breath though. Little surprise many of my Swedish friends mentioned petting and cuddling up with their pet as one of their favorite ways to njuta.

If you look at the science, it makes sense. Studies suggest interacting with animals lowers blood pressure, alleviates stress, and helps to decrease feelings of depression. And just like a kram, spending time with pets increases the level of oxytocin in your brain, helping you to feel calm.[75]

No pets at home? There's a good reason why Grumpy Cat has 2.6 million Instagram followers at the time of writing this book. Research has shown that just looking at animal pictures, memes, and videos can boost happiness. And there's nothing to stop you from dog or cat sitting or asking dog owners if you can pet their four-legged friends when you're out on a walk. It's the perfect way to tap into your senses for feel-good vibes. And you'll leave tails wagging in your wake!

CHAPTER 9

njuta

throughout the seasons

"Shared joy is a double joy; shared sorrow is half a sorrow."

—Swedish proverb

Sociologist Émile Durkheim described "collective effervescence" as the positive energy and sense of harmony you get from gathering in a large group for a common purpose.[76] Durkheim was referring to religious gatherings, but the same philosophy can apply to all kinds of group events. You may have witnessed the electric atmosphere while watching a soccer game with others and the mutual elation when your side wins, the euphoria on the dance floor when you move to the same beat as others to a favorite tune, or as Swedes note, the uplifting sensation of belting out songs in harmony with others (see page 70).

They say time flies when you're having fun (science explains this by the release of dopamine, which tricks your brain into thinking less time has passed).[77] It's therefore important to capture the pleasurable moment before it zooms by in a blur. Press pause. Breathe it in. Bathe in it. Not only will you feel an elevated sense of well-being in the moment, but it's also a snapshot in time you'll njuta from for years!

Of course, though, first you need to create these moments.

Rituals and traditions

Rituals and traditions can bind a family, culture, or nation and help to create a sense of belonging and connection. They can also be calming and comforting and bring us joy. Traditions also help us to be in the present and celebrate the important things in life.

This is not lost on our Swedish friends. A survey by the Foresight Factory, a leading consumer trends agency, revealed that a higher percentage of Swedes agreed with the statement "I love any excuse to have a celebration" than any other country in the world![78] "We have long favored a 'moments economy' approach—preferring to celebrate the small, humble things in life like *Kanelbullens Dag* (Cinnamon Bun Day)," my friend and trend expert, Stefan, explains.

Whether it's a traditional celebration that's been enjoyed for centuries or a personal take on an imported event, Swedes are there with their Valentine's Day roses, Mother's Day poems, and Halloween witch hats!

Celebrating food

Unless you're a real foodie, it's not much fun figuring out what to cook day in, day out—even if you have foraged and preserved it yourself (see page 43). But our practical Nordic friends have found the answer with designated days for different meals.

On Thursdays, it's traditional to eat pea soup and pancakes, and on Fridays tacos or tortillas are the order of the day (I'm not kidding!).

You might not like pea soup every Thursday but having a plan in place means less time thinking and more time savoring each mouthful! Should you run out of ideas, Swedes also have a long list of different foods to celebrate throughout the year:

Swedish food celebrations

Pizzadagen (International Pizza Day): January 1

Marzipanens dag (Marzipan Day): January 12

Fettisdagen (Fat Tuesday): 47 days before Easter Sunday

Morotskakansdag (Carrot Cake Day): February 3

Punschrullensdag (Marzipan Rolls Dipped in Chocolate Day): March 7

Våffeldagen (Waffle Day): March 25

Lakritsdagen (Licorice Day): April 12

Chokladbollens dag (Chocolate Ball Day): May 11

Muffin dagen (Muffin Day): May 27

Sillens dag (Herring Day): June 6

Rulltårtans dag (Swiss Roll Day): August 9

Köttbullens dag (Meatball Day): August 23

Svampens dag (Mushroom Day): September 3

Kebabens dag (Kebab Day): September 28

Kaffedagen (Coffee Day): October 1

Kanelbullens dag (Cinnamon Bun Day): October 4

Gräddtårtans dag (Whipped Cream Cake Day):
October 6

Räkmackans dag (Open Prawn Sandwich Day):
October 14

Kladdkakans dag (Swedish Mud Cake Day):
November 7

Ostkakans dag (Cheesecake Day): November 14

Wienerbrödets dag (Danish Pastry Day):
November 22

Pepparkakans dag (Gingerbread Day):December 9

Lussekatter (Saffron Bun Day): December 13

Kakans dag (Cookie Day): December 18

Celebrations through the seasons

Each new season brings exciting age-old (and new) traditions to nourish the soul and turn an average day into an exceptional day! Go that extra mile to embrace them and you'll find a way to njuta year-round. Here are a few rituals, events, and celebrations in Sweden, some of which might be new to you, others more familiar.

Spring

Vår (spring) in Sweden officially starts on March 1, although weather-wise it can feel a whole lot later! Having lived through plenty of cold, damp southern Swedish winters, spring has become my favorite season of the year!

"Everything bursts into life—the trees, the people, we feel positive and energized," my friend Carina Grefmar, a leather upholsterer, enthuses. "Spring marks the return of simple things like being able to sit outside and have a drink with a friend in the warm sunshine, rather than being cooped up indoors."

Here are few ways to celebrate spring like a Swede.

***Alla hjartans dag* (Valentine's Day)** This is a relatively new phenomenon in Sweden, having been introduced in the 1960s. Even so, February 14 is a welcome "love-in" toward the end of a somewhat cold and gloomy winter and many couples choose to celebrate it by dining out or sending a rose (more than four million are said to be sent in Sweden on this day each year!).[79] It's also a popular family celebration—and an opportunity to treat each other to sugared heart-shaped candies!

Too commercial for you? Why not make your own chocolates with a touch of raspberry (cocoa in chocolate has been found to have a mood-enhancing effect[80]) and spread a little love? Everyone will njuta from their fika a little more that day!

Koslāpp **(cow release)** In spring, the cows in Sweden are released back into the meadows after being cooped up in a barn over winter. Known as *koslāpp*, watching the cows leap and bound out onto the fresh pastures with unabashed joy has become a popular event on the calendar, and farmers hand out milk and cinnamon buns to celebrate the occasion.

Look out for fun offbeat events in your area—you'll be amazed at what's out there and you might just start a new annual tradition!

***Valborgsmässoafton* (Walpurgis Night)** Casually referred to as *Valborg*, *Valborgsmässoafton* occurs on April 30 when villagers gather at dusk around a bonfire, listen to speeches, and sing songs. The Swedish celebration was traditionally believed to ward off evil spirits, but today it presents a perfect opportunity to celebrate spring.

"I love Valborg. It's a low-key, simple celebration with a focus on togetherness," my friend Sofie explains. "It's a perfect way to rejoice that the harsh months are behind us and that brighter days lie ahead."

Have a yard? Why not reward your back-breaking efforts in your yard by inviting friends over to gather around a bonfire? You could even roast sausages or stick bread (see page 100) over the open fire!

***Påsk* (Easter)** Largely secular, Påsk is a welcome holiday in Sweden, not least because it marks the sign that summer is on its way! Garish feathers and eggs appear on bushes and children dress as *Påskkärring* (Easter witches) with brightly colored headscarves, rosy cheeks, and freckles, and go around knocking on doors in a quest for candies.

As with most Swedish celebrations, Swedes gather the day before (a tradition that predates the mechanical clock, when a new day began at sunset as opposed to midnight) on Easter Saturday, and indulge in a smorgasbord of pickled herring, poached salmon, meatballs, quiche, new potatoes with dill, crispbread, and a variety of egg dishes before heading out to see what the *Påskhare* (the Easter bunny) has left behind! There is likely to be egg painting, egg rolling, and some eggnog involved too!

Easter is the perfect time to brighten up your home with sunny yellows and vibrant pastels. Why not channel the Swedes and hand paint eggs to hang from branches indoors and attach colorful feathers to bushes outside your door for an instant spring feel? Don't forget to step back and take in the scene of the returning light, the joy on the children's faces as they hunt for eggs, and njuta from the moment.

Semlor While spring cuisine is all about delicate dishes such as salmon, asparagus, and greens, there's one exception: semlor. This wheat flour bun, filled with almond paste and a crazy amount of whipped cream, is a carb-filled classic and hugely popular—according to the Swedish Association of Bakers and

Confectioners, Swedes consume around six million each year in the lead-up to Easter, with a lion's share eaten on *Fettisdagen* (Shrove, or Fat, Tuesday)!

"Semlor are steeped in family tradition, and everyone has a special way of eating theirs," my friend Helena says. "My father used to bake them every Tuesday in the month running up to Shrove Tuesday. I love to eat it slowly and really savor every mouthful. I probably wouldn't delight in it as much if we ate them year-round."

Unless you dislike marzipan, I defy you not to love the taste of semlor! There are plenty of recipes online—and a perfect opportunity to njuta in the springtime!

Summer

It's fair to say Swedes live for summer. And after a long, dark winter, who can blame them? Summer days in Sweden are pure joy. Windows and doors are thrown open, filling the home with the sweet scent of roses, jasmines, and lilacs. Swedes spill out onto the streets, parks, porches, cliffs, and beaches to soak up every drop of golden sun.

Andy Williams's classic song might claim Christmas as "the most wonderful time of the year," but for a Swede, June, July, and August is where it's at! And it all kicks off on the summer solstice.

Midsummer Arguably the most important date in the Swedish calendar, *midsommar* (midsummer) is celebrated on the first Friday following the summer solstice.

City streets are deserted as Swedes flock to the countryside and the morning is spent picking wildflowers, which are used to make a *midsommarkrans* (floral crown), before gathering at a village maypole. If the maypole reminds you of something else, you haven't drunk too much *akvavit* (a popular Scandinavian spirit distilled from potatoes or grains and infused with various herbs and spices); the phallic symbol was originally designed to fertilize the ground to ensure a great harvest. Today, Swedes of all ages dance and hop around it, singing various songs, including one about small frogs!

A lunch of pickled herring, boiled potatoes with fresh dill, smoked salmon, and beautifully ripe strawberries is served outside no matter the weather. Every now and then everyone launches into a song, quickly followed by a shot of akvavit. And the merry gathering gets merrier by the minute!

It's a beautiful event—my favorite of all. What better way to stop and celebrate the long hours of sunshine, nature in full bloom, and togetherness?

Why not celebrate midsummer this year? It's a perfect excuse to get together for some fun and games as well as to pause and appreciate the long-awaited summer in all its glory. Do like the Swedes and scavenge the area for pretty summer flowers and make midsummer crowns. But most important of all, don't forget to stop and take inventory of your surroundings, the warmth, the light, the sounds of the birds in the trees, and the vibrancy of nature in full bloom.

Kubb

No midsummer in Sweden would be complete without a highly competitive game of *kubb*. Dating back to the early twentieth century, kubb (pronounced keb) is a lawn game on a small rectangular field. The aim of the game is to knock over *kubbar* (wooden blocks) on the opposite side of the field with *kastpinnar* (wooden batons) before knocking down the "king" in the middle. It's widely available around the world these days (in 2011, Wisconsin declared itself to be the "Kubb Capital of North America," with the city hosting the U.S. National Kubb Championship), if you'd like to have a little fun with this yard game too!

***Kräftskiva* (The Crayfish Party)** Just as the summer days start to fade and the nights draw in, Sweden is gearing up for one final hurrah before returning to work: a *kräftskiva*. The crayfish party doesn't have a specific date in the calendar, but August is the month when, historically, crayfish could be legally harvested. Today this bears little relevance—even so, it's typical to wait until the first Wednesday in August.

If you are lucky enough to be invited to a kräftskiva, you're in for a treat! Held at home or at a summer cottage, and involving family and friends, the setting is festooned with vibrant colored decorations and a "man in the moon" motif (thought to symbolize the deep orange of the August moon and a sign that the nights are becoming darker). "It's a case of the more the merrier—adults, children, dogs, everyone is welcome," furniture designer Louise Hederström explains. "It's nice to sit outdoors surrounded by nature, but if the weather doesn't allow for it, a boathouse or barn make a great backup." The laidback affair calls for a relaxed wardrobe including a bib and a conical hat (crayfish cracking is a messy affair!) . . . and an enormous amount of mosquito repellent!

The highlight, of course, is the crayfish. Prepared in brine, then decorated with crown dill, the crayfish are served with crusty bread and a Västerbotten cheese (a hard cow's milk cheese with a strong flavor, from the Västerbotten region of Sweden) pie washed down with beer and akvavit. Loudly slurping the brine from the crayfish is also a requirement, an activity occasionally interjected with singing (of course).

"It's a great way to gather to stop and celebrate the end of summer," Sofie enthuses. "There's always someone who goes skinny-dipping too." Just avoid the crayfish in the moonlight though—they might be waiting for revenge!

SIX STEPS FOR HOSTING A CRAYFISH PARTY

1. **Find a relaxed setting—preferably outdoors (think fishy odors and flying claws!).**
2. **While some Swedes might catch their own crayfish from a nearby lake, you're more likely to find them at the supermarket or a local fish market.**
3. **Decorate the table and surroundings with brightly colored red and yellow paraphernalia and ensure that each guest has a party hat and bib.**
4. **Create song sheets and encourage plenty of singing throughout the evening.**
5. **Set out the akvavit and schnapps—as any Swede will tell you, these are essential elements to the party!**
6. **Don't forget to step back while the party is in full swing to take in the revelry and njut from the moment!**

Autumn

All good things must come to an end. And as the leaves start to curl in the fading August light, Swedes reluctantly lock up their summer cottages and make their way back to the city. A new season has begun and it's about wrapping up warm and cozying up the home. Outside, the woods become an array of fiery reds, oranges, and golds. While summer is about relaxing and reflecting, autumn brings with it the opportunity to start afresh as well as live in the moment in a way that's unlike any other season.

Post-summer resolutions After a summer of quiet reflection, my Nordic friends see the start of autumn—and the return to school and work—as a time to set new goals. The reason? "As a child, autumn is a time to start a new school year with blank notebooks. As an adult, you can also use this as an opportunity for a fresh start and put all your renewed energy into exciting projects and positive life changes," Ullis explains.

> Why not use those days after you're back from your summer holiday to set new goals for a healthier, happier you? It might be as little as slowing down and finding small moments for yourself in your day to savor your surroundings.

Getting the basics right to celebrate the season As we gravitate indoors, it's time to snuggle up in soft, warm knits and *mysbyxa* (cozy trousers) to keep the cold at bay. And there's one humble item Swedes wouldn't do without: the raggsockor (wool socks)!

Traditionally knitted from reused, thick wool yarn, the humble raggsockor is a perfect way to keep your feet toasty once you've disposed of your shoes at the door (a necessity in Sweden)! Knit your own or shop online or in person and you'll have lovely warm toes throughout the season. A friend of mine keeps a basket by the door for friends so they can kick back and put their feet up in style too!

Harvest festival As the light starts to fade, nature erupts in one final hurrah, blessing the bushes, trees, and forest floors with an abundance of culinary delights ripe for the picking!

Harvest time in Sweden occurs between August and early October, and in centuries past, this meant the entire village would gather to help harvest all the crops and enjoy a *skördefestival* (harvest festival). The reward would be the abundance of apples, plums, eggplants, carrots, beans, cauliflowers, and other beautifully ripe fruits and vegetables overflowing in stores!

Today, of course, we have access to a plentiful supply of food year-round, and as the world population becomes increasingly urbanized, harvest festivals have largely fallen out of favor. Even so, skördefestival celebrations still take place around Sweden, some of which are several day events, with stalls full of food, games, and performances by local choirs (see page 70).

With the changing climate, a successful local harvest is becoming something to rejoice in once again. So why not resurrect the celebration? Grow something edible of your own, cook a dish with locally produced ingredients, or invite others over to mark the occasion and njuta from the moment.

Throw your own harvest festival

Every year, my friend Malin Persson and her family celebrate harvest time with a garden party. "We gather every autumn and enjoy a hearty root vegetable stew, followed by yard games such as sack racing and who can build the highest apple tower. It's a great way to stop and celebrate all that our surroundings provide for us, as well as pause and enjoy food at its finest, in good company."

THREE HARVEST FESTIVAL GAMES TO NJUTA FROM

1. **WHO CAN BUILD THE HIGHEST APPLE TOWER** Set a timer and see which team can build the highest tower from a basket of apples.

2. **BERRY THREADING RACE** Gather under a tree ripe with berries and provide each team with a needle and thread. Set a timer and see which team can create the longest berry chain.

3. **PUMPKIN HOOP GAME** Compete to see who can throw the most hoops over a pumpkin stem.

> ***Did you know...*** on Alla Helgons dag (All Saints Day), Swedes gather at dusk to pay tribute to loved ones by visiting their graves and lighting a candle in their honour. This beautiful tradition serves as a meaningful way to cherish memories of those we have lost while the flickering candlelight magically transforms even the gloomiest of cemeteries into a warm and inviting setting in the crisp autumn evening.

Winter

In late autumn I start to panic. Soon the cold blanket of Swedish winter will descend upon us. The landscape might be stark and largely devoid of life, but in the north, nature puts on a spectacular performance. Better than any fireworks, the *Norrsken* (Northern Lights) is a sight to behold.

Even so, as the last of the autumn leaves fall to the ground, we're looking at a very long, very dark winter, prompting an extreme desire to dive under my comforter and hide out until spring!

You might recognize a season like this in your country too, and, like me, dread this time of year. Given that the Swedish winters are some of the harshest on the globe, just how do our Nordic friends still rank high in the happiness charts and njuta from winter? The answer, my friend, is not blowing in the icy cold wind, it's down to a positive mindset and the willingness to embrace the season for what it is! I've picked up many tips and tricks along the way on how to lift the spirits and celebrate the season, and I hope they'll inspire you too!

SEVEN TIPS FOR TAKING CARE OF YOURSELF THIS WINTER

1. **INDULGE YOURSELF** Eating well is vital for energy levels and overall well-being! Treat yourself to mouthwatering in-season dishes including rich casseroles and stews—and enjoy the process of making them too. Don't forget to take vitamin D to compensate for the lack of sunlight and keep your body feeling balanced. Nordic favorites such as eggs, cheese, and fatty fish (such as tuna, salmon, and mackerel) will help do the trick! Oh, and enjoy a few sweet treats too!

2. **LOOK ON THE BRIGHT SIDE** If you approach winter worried about how dark and relentlessly cold it's going to be, you're on a slippery slope to the winter blues. Instead, approach winter with a more positive mindset, and not only will you be able to cope better, you'll njuta from it too! Swedes consider winter a mysig (cozy) time, and a season in which to rest, slow down, and enjoy the simple pleasures in life, to promote greater well-being.

3. **EVEN IF IT IS COLD, DON'T TALK ABOUT IT** A simple one, but you can quickly talk yourself into being cold. Instead, think about positive ways to describe the weather, like "invigorating," "fresh," and "crisp." It might take some practice in negative temperatures and a howling gale, although a Swede will tell you, "There's no such thing as bad weather, only bad clothing."

4. **MANAGE YOUR EXPECTATIONS** Expect the weather to be cold and gray so that every sunny day is a wonderful gift to savor!

5. **ADAPT YOUR LIFESTYLE TO THE SEASON** Reduced sunlight naturally makes us feel sleepier and more lethargic and research suggests we may need more sleep in winter.[81] It's important to embrace this. "You'll feel less energy, but while summer is a time for action, think of winter as a time for restoration," my friend Ullis advises. "By listening to your body and adapting to the weather, you'll feel more in tune and better able to cope with the season." Feel like a nap? Enjoy that slumber! Like staying in and curling up with a book? Turn those pages! Winter is a time for self-love and me time!

6. **GET OUT THERE** The darkness can make you feel lethargic, but as tempting as it is to stay indoors, Scandinavians understand the importance of frilufsliv (open air living—see page 83) and physical exercise (see page 59). Simple activities like walking, running, grilling sausages over an open fire (see page 100), and biking to work are all part of daily life, no matter the weather! Your efforts will boost your energy and your spirits, plus your home will feel even toastier when you return!

7. **GATHER ROUND** Since winter drives people indoors, it's a perfect time to get together and feel all the warmth from being surrounded by loved ones! "No one likes to linger in wintertime, everyone is rushing to get back into the warmth of their home. This means many natural interactions stop," my friend Malin Nihlberg explains. "It's so important to arrange lots of dates with friends and family. It's a great way to keep your spirits up!"

Lucia, the bearer of light By December 13, it's dark in Sweden. It's *very* dark. But the Swedes have a plan. St. Lucia, a Sicilian saint who is fabled for poking her own eyes out rather than marrying her suitor, has been adopted and turned into a surprisingly heartwarming annual Swedish celebration of light!

Kicking off before dawn, tradition dictates that the eldest daughter in the house appears in a white dress with a red sash, singing a melancholy song and wearing a crown of candles in her hair while bearing coffee, *lussebulle* (saffron buns), and gingerbread. Later that morning, celebrations involving a *Luciatåg* (Lucia procession) take place across the country. It's a magical procession of light, brightening up the darkness and bringing a touch of joy to the dark month of December . . . even if everyone is a little bleary-eyed in the beginning!

Why not join in the celebration by baking traditional lightly sweet saffron buns? There are plenty of recipes to follow online!

Christmas

Although Christmas occurs during winter, it's such an important tradition in Sweden and comes with so many of its own customs that the period leading up to Christmas is essentially considered a season of its own. Despite less than 2 percent of Swedes attending church regularly,[82] many embrace *Jul* (Christmas), which they see as a perfect excuse to add much needed warmth and coziness to their homes. It's therefore an important time of year that is full of tradition.

Just how do Swedes maximize njutning from the yuletide period? It's all down to taking a little extra effort, keeping things simple, and making a conscious decision to savor the small moments throughout the entire period, not just the big day. With studies indicating that Christmas rituals like decorating, baking, and crafting fill us with meaning, help to restore calm[83] (much needed at this time of year), and evoke well-being,[84] who are we to argue?

Here are some ways that Swedes slow down and tap into the joy, warmth, and nostalgia of the holiday period so it doesn't zoom by in a blur.

Mindful Christmas decorating

In Sweden, the First Sunday of Advent marks the start of Christmas, and the day is set aside for important yuletide rituals. Homes spring to life as paper star lanterns, *snöblommor* (snow flowers), and traditional *adventsljusstake* (inverted V-shaped candleholders) are hauled from the attic and set up in the windows. Advent candles are lit, and some might go off to a *glöggmingel* (Christmas drinks party), while others host their own.

But not all decorations appear right away. Swedes take a slow approach, adding small festive touches throughout December.

Start early and take your time to decorate, layering your home over time, rather than doing everything at once. It will feel more mindful and less of a chore. Plus, you'll be able to njuta from each update even more!

Fill your home with the scent of Christmas

Forget garish; in Sweden decorations tend to be an understated, multisensory affair, heavily drawing on nature. Think branches of pine, a homemade boxwood or eucalyptus wreath, as well as bulbs of hyacinths and amaryllises wrapped in moss, Christmas tree saplings in vases, sometimes decorated with a single bauble, and dried orange garlands hanging in the kitchen, filling the home with the wonderful scent of the season. And, of course, there are candles everywhere, bathing the rooms in a warm and soothing glow. And finally, the home is filled with the wonderful scent of pine from a freshly chopped tree!

Scent is a great way to trigger memories.[86] Filling your home with divine smelling decorations from nature helps to awaken happy memories from Christmases past! Furthermore, studies have found those who stop and savor positive memories report greater overall happiness in the present.[87] So, keep it natural and fill your home with the wonderful scent of Christmas!

Julpyssla *(Christmas crafting)*

Swedes love to set aside time for julpyssla especially if they have young ones at home. It's a great way to pause and do something mindful together or alone, plus you'll njuta from the results!

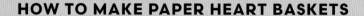

HOW TO MAKE PAPER HEART BASKETS

My children have been making traditional woven paper heart baskets since their *dagis* (preschool) days. They make a great pouch for homemade candies and add a personal touch to gifts or as decoration on the tree. Here's how to spread a little love this Jul.

WHAT YOU NEED

- Pen or pencil
- Paper (any kind—plain, colored, wallpaper, leftover gift paper—will do!)
- Scissors
- Glue

STEPS

1. Trace or copy the template onto two different styles of paper and cut out the template with scissors.
2. Fold in half along the dotted line.
3. Cut along each solid line.
4. Reverse the paper so the template lines aren't visible from the outside.
5. Position the two templates to form an overlapping right angle to form a heart shape.

6. Start with one section and weave it through the corresponding section of the other template.

7. Continue with the next section, weaving it through in the opposite direction. Continue until your templates are woven together.

8. Cut out a long rectangular strip of paper and attach it to the top of each side of the heart with glue to form a handle.

9. Fill your heart basket with candies or other goodies and hang it from the tree.

PAPER HEART BASKET TEMPLATE

Love to bake?

Along with crafting, many Swedes love to set aside an afternoon for making all kinds of Christmas delights! Gingerbread houses, *smörkola* (a type of caramel not dissimilar from toffee or fudge), and *knäck* (Christmas butterscotch) are all part of the repertoire. It's a great way to slow down, take time for yourself, and fill the home with the wonderful scent of Christmas! And, of course, once your work is done, nothing warms the heart like a steaming mug of *glögg* (spiced mulled wine) and freshly baked gingerbread by the tree in your *raggsockor* (see page 208).

221

Julkalendern
(Christmas Calendar)

Between December 1 and 24, more than two million Swedes curl up on the sofa to watch the television program *Julkalendern*. Made up of fifteen-minute-long daily episodes, the series follows a different mystery or adventure each year, with a finale on Christmas Eve. At the end of each episode, there's a televised segment to show the opening of the day's advent calendar. Many back home buy the same calendar—which is widely available and contains images related to that day's storyline—and open the window at the same time.

"December can be a stressful time, and *Julkalendern* offers an excuse to press the pause button for fifteen minutes in the early evening, cozy up under a blanket with the family, and enjoy a traditional Christmas activity," my friend Helena explains.

You might not have a series like this to watch, but set aside time each day to snuggle up and njuta.

Christmas bucket list

It's all very well suggesting decorating, baking, and crafting, but with the endless preparations surrounding this time of year, your head might just begin to spin! Enter the Christmas bucket list.

"Each member of our family chooses one thing they would *really* like to do around Christmas—whether it's baking Christmas sweets, going to a [Christmas] carol concert, or sledding in the park," explains Helena. "By breaking it down to one activity per person, it takes the pressure off and makes it easier to plan a Christmas that everyone can njuta from."

What will be on your Christmas bucket list?

Christmas wrapping and rhymes

The most important touch on Swedes' beautifully wrapped presents is the rhyme! On *Lille Julafton* (Little Christmas Eve, the day before Christmas Eve), it's time to sit down quietly and *rimma* (write rhymes). It's a longstanding Swedish tradition—and that one Per's family takes very seriously! The rhyme should be short and witty and hint at what's inside, without giving it away. I love the idea as it makes present giving a slower, personal, and more thoughtful affair! Worth a try?

The big day

After all the decorating, baking, wrapping, and writing rhymes, the big day finally arrives: *Julafton* (Christmas Eve). Up and down the country, Swedes gather as a family, partaking in a traditional *Julbord* (Christmas table) bursting with pickled herring, shellfish, salmon, eggs, red and green cabbage, sausages, meatballs, *ris à la Malta* (rice pudding), and many other delicacies. It's a relaxed, joyous affair, made all the merrier by *snappsvisor* (schnapps songs), which are sung with gusto!

While the day might be lots of fun and steeped in family tradition—including a mandatory viewing of the 1958 *Walt Disney Presents Christmas* special "From All of Us to All of You" at 3:00 p.m., and a visit from *Tomten* (Father Christmas)—the real njuta comes from taking a moment to step back and soak up the Christmas cheer. "I njuter from the smiles on my children's faces, the laughter, the games, and the togetherness of it all," Per says. But most of all, I think he takes the greatest njutning from his father's homemade *punsch* (a form of liqueur)!

It's easy to get wrapped up in a frenzy of gift paper, cooking a massive turkey with all the trimmings, and all the other things happening on Christmas Day, and before you know it, the day's over. But if you actively stop and take a moment for yourself to simply observe, soak up the atmosphere, and take in the spirit of the moment, time will stand still if only for a moment.

Celebrating the end of Christmas

While in many parts of Europe, it's considered unlucky to keep your decorations up past Twelfth Night (January 6), I break into a sweat each year as the date sails past in Sweden and the decorations remain until *tjugondedag jul* (twenty days after Christmas).

The tradition derives from the time of King Kanut, when children would run around the village to *ropa ut julen* (shout out Christmas) on January 13, letting everyone know that Christmas had ended, and beg for food and drink. In the twentieth century, it became popular for private homes, schools, and churches to throw a Knut's party or Knut's dance in which they sing and dance around a tree. *Julgransplundring* (to loot the tree) of all its ornaments and eat any edible decorations is also an important part of the day. In some homes, children also smash gingerbread houses and devour them.

"Julgransplundring is one of my favorite days of the year," an acquaintance Maria Ohlson Andersson tells me. "In our house we throw a family party, give out magazines and candies, sing songs and physically throw the tree out of the door!"

I have to say, it all sounds a little "bah, humbug" now to simply pack up the decorations and put them back in the attic. Something to think about for next year?

A reflective New Year's Eve

Shortly after Christmas comes New Year's Eve, which brings the Christmas season to a close. It's so easy to get wrapped up in New Year's Eve celebrations that often you forget yourself in the process. The final day of the year is an ideal time for quiet reflection, grounding yourself before the clock strikes midnight. For some, like my husband and youngest daughter, a vinterbad (winter dip) (see page 116) is the perfect way to clear the cobwebs. For others, like myself, it might be a stroll alone along the beach before the celebrations begin.

The reflection doesn't need to stop there. My friend Malin Persson makes up her family's *Nyårsafton* (New Year's Eve) menu with ingredients they've preserved through the seasons (think homegrown artichokes for the starter and the last berries of autumn to accompany dessert), creating a culinary journey, with each mouthful taking them back to a cherished moment in the year.

And when midnight arrives everyone heads out to watch the fireworks brighten up the night sky, as a new year rolls in with a bang!

A new year also signifies a great opportunity for a fresh start. According to Statista, America's top New Year's resolutions for 2023 were to exercise more (52 percent), eat healthier (50 percent), lose weight (40 percent), and save money (39 percent). All important goals, but I can't help thinking a year of training and dieting sounds a little heavy! It's hardly surprising only 9 percent successfully complete their goals for the year![88]

But how about "Swedifying" each of these for greater success? Instead of the vague "exercise more," take a lesson from the Swedish lifestyle and plan to incorporate exercise into your daily life and/or vow to take up a sports/activities that you truly enjoy.

Rather than associating "eating healthier" with dieting, how about aiming to eat more local, in-season, nutrition-rich food, making meals from scratch, slowing down, and savoring every mouthful more?

And finally, Swedes have taught me it's important to focus not just on your physical well-being but on your mental well-being too. Make this the year you put your needs first and give yourself a little self-love.

Epilogue

As I rush from place to place, usually just barely keeping up, I've often admired how the Swedes around me march to the beat of their own drum, taking their time to do things right. And yet they still seem to get just as much done. Possibly more!

As I delved deeper into the intricacies of the word "njuta" while writing this book, I realized how easy it is to let the little pleasures in life pass us by, postponing happiness, and believing *livsglädje* (the joy of life) will follow once we're finally sitting on a deck chair sipping a mojito, or we've made our first (second, third . . .) million.

But listening to my Swedish friends and family, I have learned that by making a conscious effort to stop and seize small moments throughout the day, to be present and indulge the senses—no matter how fleeting—we can turn the ordinary into something extraordinary.

Many Swedes suggest resistance is key, and the more effort you put in, the higher the reward; they cite exercise, or even sleeping out under the open sky, a vinterbad (an outdoor dip in winter) or even completing the arduous, sweat-inducing Swedish Classic challenge as examples.

But my Nordic friends have also taught me that it doesn't need to be complicated. Simple conscious actions like angling your face up to the sun to catch its warm rays or savoring the taste of the first juicy red strawberry of the season can do wonders to lift your spirits on the dullest of days.

So the next time you're rushing around, stop and remember the wise words of the Swedes: *Ta det lungt* (take it easy), *det är ingen ko på isen* (there's no cow on the ice). Njut! Because *det är du värd* (you are worth it)!

Acknowledgments

I am so grateful to all the Swedes who so gracefully gave up their time to share personal experiences of the word "njuta" with me. Specifically: Helena, with whom I share my studio and whom I bugged every ten minutes with random questions about Swedish culture (you're a fountain of knowledge). To dear friends Ullis, Sofie, Tove, Sarah, Emma, Mattias, Tina, Malin Persson, Malin Nihlberg, Maria, Carina, Nina, Lucas (as well as Alma, Tuva, Edith) and Bettina, and many more who took the time to drink coffee and eat cinnamon buns with me while I grilled you on everything from cold-water swimming to the colors in your home and what you take with you to the forest: *Tack så mycket* (thank you so much)!

A big thank-you also to my husband, Per, stepson, Albin, and daughters Olivia and Alice, who put up with my excessively loud typing at all hours of the day and for teaching me about the powers of being present. You are my world. Also to Johan, Christina, Inger, and Bo as well as Cas, Charlie, and my mother. And in loving memory of my father, who truly knew how to savor the simple things in life.

Last but by no means least, I'd like to extend my gratitude to my wonderful publishing team at HarperCollins, including Marta Schooler, who trusted in my idea, Jenna Lefkowitz for being a fantastic editor, and Lynne Yeamans and Stephanie Stislow for design—without whom this book would never have been possible.

Notes

1   Bryant, Fred, "Current Progress and Future Directions for Theory and Research on Savoring." *Frontiers of Psychology*, no. 12 (December 14, 2021): 1-17. https://doi.org/10.3389/fpsyg.2021.771698

2   Ramirez-Duran, Daniela. "Savoring in Positive Psychology: 21 Tools to Appreciate Life." PositivePsychology.com. February 5, 2021. https://positivepsychology.com/savoring/

3   Ray, Julie. "World Unhappier, More Stressed Out Than Ever." News.gallup.com. June 28, 2022. https://news.gallup.com/poll/394025/world-unhappier-stressed-ever.aspx

4   NORC at the University of Chicago. "Covid Response Tracking Study." https://www.norc.org/Research/Projects/Pages/covid-response-tracking-study.aspx

5   Gallup. "Gallup Global Emotions 2022. PDF 2022." https://www.gallup.com/analytics/349280/gallup-global-emotions-report.aspx?thank-you-report-form=1

6   Smith, Jennifer, and Agnieszka Hanni. "Effects of a Savoring Intervention on Resilience and Well-being of Older Adults." *Journal of Applied Gerontology* 38, no. 1 (January 2019): 137-152. https://doi.org/10.1177/0733464817693375

7   Cherry, Kendra. "What Is the Negativity Bias." Verywellmind.com. November 14, 2022. https://www.verywellmind.com/negative-bias-4589618

8   Dixon, S. "Average Daily Time Spent on Social Media Worldwide 2012-2022." Statista. August 22, 2022. https://www.statista.com/statistics/433871/daily-social-media-usage-worldwide/

9   Ophir, Eyal, Clifford Nass, and Anthony Wagner. "Cognitive Control in Media Multitaskers." *Proceedings of the National Academy of Sciences of the United States of America* 106, no. 37 (July 20, 2009: 15583-87. https://doi.org/10.1073/pnas.0903620106

10 Bowker, Julie, Miriam Stotsky, and Rebecca Etkin. "How BIS/BAS and Psycho-behavioral Variables Distinguish Between Social Withdrawal Subtypes During Emerging Adulthood." *Personality and Individual Differences* 119 (December 1, 2017): 283-288, https://doi.org/10.1016/j.paid.2017.07.043

11 Leontiev, Dmitry. "The Dialectics of Aloneness: Positive vs. Negative Meaning and Differential Assessment." *Counselling Psychology Quarterly* 32, no. 3-4 (July 9, 2019): 548-62, https://doi.org/10.1080/09515070.2019.1640186

12 Finke, Brian. "The Work Issue. Failure to Launch: The Lamentable Rise of Desktop Dining." *New York Times*, February 25, 2016. https://www.nytimes.com/2016/02/28/magazine/failure-to-lunch.html

13 Schlosser, Eric. "Americans Are Obsessed with Fast Food: The Dark Side of the All-American Meal." CBS News. January 31, 2002. https://cbsnews.com/news/americans-are-obsessed-with-fast-food-the-dark-side-of-the-all-american-meal/

14 Quoidbach, Jordi, and Elizabeth Dunn. "Give It Up: A Strategy for Combating Hedonic Adaptation." *Social Psychological and Personality Science*, 4, no. 5 (January 31, 2013): 563–68. https://doi.org/10.1177/1948550612473489

15 Ramirez-Duran, Daniela. "Savoring Positive Pscyhology: 21 Tools to Appreciate Life." PositivePsychology.com (February 5, 2021). https://positivepsychology.com/savoring/

16 Moreno-Agostino et al. "Mediterranean Diet and Wellbeing: Evidence from a Nationwide Survey." *Psychology & Health* 34, no. 3, (October 15, 2018): 321-35. https://doi.org/10.1080/08870446.2018.1525492

17 Meininger's International. "Sweden's Love Affair with the Bag-in-box." September 8, 2014. https://www.wine-business-international.com/wine/general/swedens-love-affair-bag-box

18 Bernard, Kristine. "The Top Coffee-Consuming Countries." *WorldAtlas*. August 6 2020. https://www.worldatlas.com/articles/top-10-coffee-consuming-nations

19 Luko. "Global Bicycle Cities Index 2022." January 16, 2023. https://de.luko.eu/en/advice /guide/bike-index/

20 Department of Transport. "National Travel Survey:2020." September 22, 2021. https://www. gov.uk/government/statistics/national-travel-survey-2020/national-travel-survey-2020

21 Althoff et al. "Large-scale Physical Activity Data Reveal Worldwide Activity Inequality." *Nature* 547, no. 7663 (July 20, 2017): 336-39. https://doi.org/10.1038/nature23018

22 Bryant, Fred, Joseph Veroff. *Savoring: A New Model of Positive Experience*. Lawrence Erlbaum Associates Publishers, 2007.

23 European Commission. "Sport and Physical Activity." Eurobarometer. April-May 2022. https://europa.eu/eurobarometer/surveys/detail/2668

24 Armbrecht et al. "Swedish Sports Clubs and Events During the Covid-19 Pandemic: Impacts and Responses." In *Crisis and Recovery for Events: Impacts and Strategies* edited by Vassilios Ziakas et al., 193-212. Goodfellow Publishers, 2021.

25 Fancourt, Daisy, Lisa Aufegger, and Aaron Williamon. "Low-stress and High-stress Singing Have Contrasting Effects on Glucocorticoid Response." *Frontiers of Psychology*, no. 6 (September 4, 2015): 1-5. https://doi.org/10.3389/fpsyg.2015.01242

26 Fancourt et al. "Group Singing in Bereavement: Effects on Mental Health, Self-efficacy, Self-esteem and Well-being." *BMJ Supportive & Palliative Care* 12, no. 4 (October 2022): e607-15. https://spcare.bmj.com/content/early/2019/06/26/bmjspcare-2018-001642

27 Kreutz et al. "Effects of Choir Singing or Listening on Secretory Immunoglobulin A, Cortisol, and Emotional State." *Journal of Behavioral Medicine* 27 (December 2004): 623-35. https://doi.org/10.1007/s10865-004-0006-9

28 Dunbar et al. "Performance of Music Elevates Pain Threshold and Positive Affect: Implications for the Evolutionary Function of Music." *Evolutionary Psychology* 10, no. 4 (October 1, 2012): 688-702. https://doi.org/10.1177/147470491201000403

29 Ojay Alise, and Edzard Ernst. "Can Singing Exercises Reduce Snoring? A Pilot Study." *Complement Therapies in Medicine* 8, no. 3. (September 2000): 151-56. https://doi.org/10.1054/ctim.2000.0376

30 Kraus, Nina, and Jessica Slater, "Chapter 12—Music and Language: Relations and Disconnections." *Handbook of Clinical Neurology* 129 (February 26, 2015): 207-22. https://doi.org/10.1016/B978-0-444-62630-1.00012-3

31 de Witte, Martina et al. "Music Therapy for Stress Reduction: A Systematic Review and M-analysis." *Health Psychology Review* 16, no. 1, (November 27, 2020): 134-59. https://doi.org/10.1080/17437199.2020.1846580

32 Ferguson, Yuna, and Kennon Sheldon. "Trying to be Happier Really Can Work: Two Experimental Studies, *The Journal of Positive Psychology* 8, no. 1 (December 19, 2012): 23-33, httos://doi.org/10.1080/17439760.2012.747000

33 Gold et al. "Musical Reward Prediction Errors Engage the Nucleus Accumbens and Motivate Learning." *PNAS* 116, no. 8 (February 6, 2019): 3310-15. https://doi.org/10.1073 /pnas.1809855116

34 Corkhill, Betsan. *Knit for Health & Wellness: How to Knit a Flexible Mind and More . . . .* Flatbear Publishing, 2014.

35 Kurtz, Jaime. "Seeing Through New Eyes: An Experimental Investigation of the Benefits of Photography." *Journal of Basic & Applied Sciences*, 11 (June 3, 2015): 354-58. https://doi.org/10.6000/1927-5129.2015.11.51

36 Rizzolo, Denise et al. "Stress Management Strategies for Students: The Immediate Effects of Yoga, Humor, and Reading on Stress." *Journal of College Teaching and Learning*, 6, no. 8 (December 1, 2009): 79-88. https://doi.org/10.19030/tlc.v6i8.1117

37 O'Neill, A. "Urbanization in Sweden 2021." March 10 2023. https://www.statista.com/statistics/455935/urbanization-in-sweden/

38 Folkhälsomyndigheten. "Friluftsliv." March 4, 2022.

39 Center for Sustainable Systems, University of Michigan. 2022. "U.S. Cities Factsheet." September 2022. Pub. No. CSS09-06. https://css.umich.edu/publications/factsheets/built-environment/us-cities-factsheet

40 United Nations, Department of Economic and Social Affairs, Population Dynamics. "World Urbanization Prospects." 2018. https://population.un.org/wup/Download/

41 Bentley, Phoebe, et al. "Nature, Smells, and Human Wellbeing." *Ambio* 52, (July 18, 2022): 1-14. https://doi.org/10.1007/s13280-022-01760-w

42 The World Bank. "Forest Area (% of Land Area)—Sweden." 2023. https://data.worldbank.org/indicator/AG.LND.FRST.ZS?location=SE

43 Bentley, Phoebe, et al. "Nature, Smells, and Human Wellbeing." *Ambio* 52, (July 18, 2022): 1-14. https://doi.org/10.1007/s13280-022-01760-w

44 Bernard, Kristine. "The Top Coffee-Consuming Countries." *WorldAtlas*. August 6, 2020. https://worldatlas.com/articles/top-10-coffee-consuming-nations.html

45 Das, Gautam Kumar. "Environmental Hazards for Lockdown and Social Distancing in the COVID-19 Crisis." *Indian Science Cruiser* 35, no. 3, (May 2021): 9-25. https://www.researchgate.net/publication/353196125_Environmental_Hazards_for_Lockdown_and_Social_Distancing_in_the_COVID-19_Crisis

46 Cox, Daniel, et. al. "Doses of Neighborhood Nature: The Benefits for Mental Health of Living with Nature." *BioScience* 67, no. 2, (February 2017) 147–55, https://doi.org/10.1093/biosci/biw173

47 Nature Travels: The Outdoor Specialists. "Wildlife in Sweden." 2023. https://www.naturetravels.co.uk/wildlife.htm

48 Sweden Institute. "Here Are a Few Things to Know Before Heading Out into Sweden's Wilderness Areas." June 1, 2021. https://sweden.se/climate/nature/how-to-survive-in-swedish-nature

49 Ramirez-Duran, Daniela. "Savoring Positive Psychology: 21 Tools to Appreciate Life." PositivePsychology.com (February 5, 2021). https://positivepsychology.com/savoring/

50 Glenny, Helen. "'Cold Water Swimming: Why an Icy Dip Is Good for Your Mental and Physical Health." *BBC Science Focus*. July 24, 2020. https://www.sciencefocus.com/the-human-body/cold-water-swimming-why-an-icy-dip-is-good-for-your-mental-and-physical-health/

51 Huttunen, Pirkko, Leena Kokko, and Virpi Ylijukuri. "Winter Swimming Improves General Well-being." *International Journal of Circumpolar Health* 63, no. 2, (June 1, 2004): 140-44. https://doi.org/10.3402/ijch.v63i2.17700

52 Siems, Werner, et al. "Improved Antioxidative Protection in Winter Swimmers." *QJM: An International Journal of Medicine*, 92, no. 4, (April 1, 1999): 193-98. https://doi.org/10.1093/qjmed/92.4.193

53 Jesumani, Valentina, et al. "Potential Use of Seaweed Bioactive Compounds in Skincare—a Review." *Marine Drugs* 17, no. 12, (December 6, 2019): 688. https://doi.org/10.3390/md17120688

54 Wikipedia. "Nordic Folkboat." January 13, 2023. https://en.wikipedia.org/wiki/Nordic _Folkboat

55 Marvin. "Designing for Happier, Healthier Living at Home." April 2020. https://www.marvin.com/project-gallery/designing-for-happier-healthier-living-at-home

56 Swedish Institute. "Swedish Design Movement Presents Woodlife Sweden: Meet the Architects at Archtober." October 20, 2020. https://si.se/en/woodlife -sweden-meet-the-architects-during-archtober/

57 Muilu-Mäkelä, Riina. "Wood for Good (W4G)." Luonnonvarakeskus. June 15, 2021. https://jukuri.luke.fi/bitstream/handle/10024/547641/Wood_for_good_%28W4G%29 _loppuraportti_17.6.2021.pdf?sequence=1&isAllowed-y

58 Ikei Harumi, Chorong Song, and Yoshifumi Miyazaki. "Physiological Effects of Touching Wood." *International Journal of Environmental Research Public Health* 14, no. 7, (July 18, 2017): 801. https://doi.org/10.3390/ijerph14070801

59 Warrenburg, Stephen. "Effects of Fragrance on Emotions: Moods and Physiology." *Chemical Senses* 30, supplement 1, (January 1, 2005): i248-49. https://doi.org/10.1093/ chemse/bjh208

60 Marvin. "Designing Homes for the Power of Natural Light." December 28, 2018. https://www.marvin.com/blog/the-power-of-light

61 Ramirez-Duran, Daniela. "Savoring in Positive Psychology: 21 Tools to Appreciate Life." PositivePsychology.com (February 5, 2021). https://positivepsychology.com/savoring/

62 Bakker Iris, et al. "Color Preferences for Different Topics in Connection to Personal Characteristics." *Color Research and Application* 40, no. 1, (October 30, 2013): 62-71. https://doi.org/10.1002/col.21845

63 HTC Corporation. "HTC Reseach Reveals Good Design Makes Us Happy." February 24, 2014. https://www.htc.com/mea-en/newsroom/2014-02-24-4/

64 Minuzzo, Bridgette. "A Room with a View Provides Visual Relief for a Work-Weary Brain." University of South Australia. September 11, 2019. https://www.unisa.edu.au/Media -Centre/Releases/2019/a-room-with-a-view-provides-visual-relief-for-a-work-weary-brain/

65 Bryant, Fred, Colette Smart, and Scott King. "Using the Past to Enhance the Present: Boosting Happiness Through Positive Reminiscence." *Journal of Happiness Studies* 6 (September 2005): 227-60. https://doi.org/10.1007/s10902-005-3889-4

66 Keeney, Jessica. "Savoring Success: Effects of Basking and Acknowledgement of Others in Response to Achievement." Master's thesis, Michigan State University, 2009. https://doi.org/doi:10.25335/M5JD4PW9Z

67 Pieniazek, Jen. "Americans Left Out with Lack of Leave." *HR Future*. May 17, 2021. https:// www.hrfuture.net/talent-management/culture/americans-left-out-with-lack-of-leave/

68 U.S. Travel Association. "State of American Vacation 2018." January 2018. https://www. ustravel.org/sites/default/files/media_root/document/2018_Research_State%20of%20 American%20Vacation%202018.pdf

69 Gump, Brooks, and Karen Matthews. "Are Vacations Good for Your Health? The 9-year Mortality Experience After the Multiple Risk Factor Intervention Trial." *Psychosomatic Medicine* 65, no. 5, (September 2000): 608-12. https://doi.org/10.1097/00006842 -2000090000-00003

70 Chikani, Vatsal, et al. "Vacations Improve Mental Health Among Rural Women: The Wisconsin Rural Women's Health Study." *WMJ* 104, no. 6, (August 2005): 20-3. https://www.researchgate.net/publication/7548396_Vacations_improve_mental_health _among_rural_women_the_Wisconsin_Rural_Women%27s_Health_Study

71 Gielan, Michelle. "Planning Travel Creates Happiness." *Institute for Applied Positive Research*. August 2020. https://wwww.ustravel.org/sites/default/files/media_root

/document/PlanningTravel_MichelleGielan.pdf?utm_source=MagnetMail&utm_medium
=email&utm_content=9%2E8%2E20%2DPress%2DLGTConsumer&utm_campaign=pr

72 Light, Kathleen, Karen Grewen, and Janet Amico. "More Frequent Partner Hugs
and Higher Oxytocin Levels Are Linked to Lower Blood Pressure and Heart Rate in
Premenopausal Women." *Biological Psychology* 69, no. 1, (April 2005): 5-21.
https://doi.org/10.1016/j.biopsyhco.2004.11.002

73 Esch, Tobias, and George Stefano. "The Neurobiology of Love." *Neuro Endocrinol Letters*
26, no. 3, (June 2005): 175-92. https://pubmed.ncbi.nlm.nih.gov/15990719/

74 Healthline. "16 Reasons to Smooch: How Kissing Benefits Your Health." July 25, 2018.
https://www.healthline.com/health/benefits-of-kissing#happy-hormones

75 Beetz, Andrea, et al. "Psychosocial and Psychophysiological Effects of Human-Animal
Interactions: The Possible Role of Oxytocin." *Frontiers of Psychology*, no. 3 (July 9, 2012):
1-15. https://doi.org/10.3389/fpsyg.2012.00234

76 Durkheim, Émile. *The Elementary Forms of the Religious Life*. Library of Alexandria, 1954.

77 Simen, Patrick, and Matthew Matell. "Why Does Time Seem to Fly When We're Having Fun?"
Science 354, no. 6317, (December 9, 2016): 1231-32. https://doi.org/10.1126/science.aal4021

78 Sapsted, Georgina. "Foresight Factory's Predictions for 2025." *Foresight Factory*.
January 29, 2018. https://www.foresightfactory.co/3-predictions-for-2025/

79 The Local SE. "Top Ten Reasons to Love (or Hate) Valentine's Day in Sweden."
February 14, 2013. https://www.thelocal.se/20130214/46174/

80 Shin, Ji-Hee, et al. "Consumption of 85% Cocoa Dark Chocolate Improves Mood in
Association with Gut Microbial Changes in Healthy Adults: A Randomized Controlled
Trial." *Journal of Nutritional Biochemistry* 99, no. 108854 (August 10, 2021): 1-8.
https://doi.org/10.1016/j.jnutbio.2021.108854

81 Seidler, Aileen, et al. "Seasonality of Human Sleep: Polysomnographic Data of a
Neuropsychiatric Sleep Clinic. *Frontiers in Neuroscience* 17 (February 17, 2023).
https://doi.org/10.3389/fnins.2023.1105233

82 Commisceo Global Consulting Ltd. "Afghanistan—Language, Culture, Customs
and Etiquette." 2002. https://commisceo-global.com/resources/country-guides
/afghanistan- guide

83 Wood Brooks, Alison, et al. "Don't Stop Believing: Rituals Improve Performance by
Decreasing Anxiety." *Organizational Behavior and Human Decision Processes* 137
(November 2016): 71-85. https://doi.org/10.1016/j.obhdp.2016.07.004

84 Páez, Darío, et al. "Merry Christmas and Happy New Year! The Impact of Christmas Rituals
on Subjective Well-being and Family's Emotional Climate." *International Journal of Social
Psychology* 26, no. 3, (January 23, 2014): 373-86. https://doi.org/10.1174/021347411797361347

85 Hougaard, Anders, et al. "Evidence of a Christmas Spirit Network in the Brain: Functional
MRI Study." *BMJ* 2015;351:h6266, (December 16, 2015). https://doi.org/10.1136/bmj.h6266

86 Gottfried, Jay, et al. "Remembrance of Odors Past, Human Olfactory Cortex in
Cross-Modal Recognition Memory." *Neuron* 42, no. 4, (May 27, 2004): 687-95.
https://doi.org/10.1016/S0896-6273(04)00270-3

87 Bryant, Fred, Colette Smart, and Scott King. "Using the Past to Enhance the Present:
Boosting Happiness Through Positive Reminiscence. *Journal of Happiness Studies* 6
(September 2005): 227-260. https://doi.org/10.1007/s10902-005-3889-4

88 de Boer, Mick. "19 Mind-blowing New Year's Resolution Statistics (2023)." *InsideOut
Mastery: Unleash Your Potential*. November 15, 2022. https://insideoutmastery.com
/new-years-resolution-statistics/

Index

Niki Brantmark (née Adams) is a journalist, stylist, and the founder of My Scandinavian Home (myscandinavianhome.com), an award-winning design and lifestyle platform inspired by her life in Malmö, Sweden, where she lives with her husband and three children. Originally from London, Niki has a master's degree in psychology from the University of Edinburgh and is the author of the popular books *Lagom: The Swedish Art of Living a Balanced, Happy Life*, *The Scandinavian Home*, and *Relaxed Rustic*.

www.myscandinavianhome.com
Instagram.com/myscandinavianhome